India–Pakistan Wars and the Kashmir Crisis

T0299969

This book examines the origins of the conflict between two nuclear powers – India and Pakistan – and the instability and violence in the disputed territory of Kashmir. It presents to its readers a chronology of events and political decisions that have led to an intractable situation at present, many decades since the stand-off between India and Pakistan started.

Rathnam Indurthy traces the origins of the constant war-like situation between the two most powerful nuclear powers in South Asia through war and peace, agreements and talks, and political leaders and generals. From Indira Gandhi to Vajpayee, and from Zia-ul-Haq, Parvez Musharraf and Nawaz Sharif, the volume lays bare the various machinations on the political chessboard. It also looks at the internal issues and politics of Kashmir and offers explanations as well as solutions for the resolution of the festering impasse the two nations have reached.

This volume will be of great interest to scholars and readers of foreign policy, international relations, South Asian politics, and defense and strategic studies.

Rathnam Indurthy is Professor of Political Science at McNeese State University, Lake Charles, Louisiana, USA.

India–Pakistan Wars and the Kashmir Crisis

Rathnam Indurthy

Routledge
Taylor & Francis Group

LONDON AND NEW YORK

First published 2019
by Routledge
2 Park Square, Milton Park, Abingdon, Oxon OX14 4RN

and by Routledge
605 Third Avenue, New York, NY 10017

First issued in paperback 2020

Routledge is an imprint of the Taylor & Francis Group, an informa business

Copyright © 2019 Rathnam Indurthy

The right of Rathnam Indurthy to be identified as author of this work
has been asserted by him in accordance with sections 77 and 78 of the
Copyright, Designs and Patents Act 1988.

All rights reserved. No part of this book may be reprinted or reproduced or
utilised in any form or by any electronic, mechanical, or other means, now
known or hereafter invented, including photocopying and recording, or in
any information storage or retrieval system, without permission in writing
from the publishers.

Trademark notice: Product or corporate names may be trademarks or
registered trademarks, and are used only for identification and explanation
without intent to infringe.

British Library Cataloguing-in-Publication Data
A catalogue record for this book is available from the British Library

Library of Congress Cataloging-in-Publication Data
Names: Indurthy, Rathnam, 1940– author.
Title: India-Pakistan wars and the Kashmir crisis / Rathnam
   Indurthy. Description: Abingdon, Oxon ; New York, NY :
   Routledge, 2019. | Includes bibliographical references.
Identifiers: LCCN 2018056841 | ISBN 9780367175054 (hardback :
   alk. paper) | ISBN 9780429198854 (e-book)
Subjects: LCSH: Jammu and Kashmir (India)—Politics and
   government. | India—Foreign relations—Pakistan. | Pakistan—
   Foreign relations—India.
Classification: LCC DS485.K27 I54 2019 | DDC 327.5405491—dc23
LC record available at https://lccn.loc.gov/2018056841

ISBN 13: 978-0-367-73170-0 (pbk)
ISBN 13: 978-0-367-17505-4 (hbk)

Typeset in Times New Roman
by Apex CoVantage, LLC

Dedicated to my late mother-in-law, Mrs P.H. Chary, who lived an exemplary and inspiring life.

Contents

Preface

British India was partitioned into two independent nations – India and Pakistan – in 1947 based on the principle of religion. Ever since the partition, the state of Jammu and Kashmir, with a predominantly Muslim population, has become a bone of contention between these two countries. This contention has led to a series of wars and crises since 1947 that continues to the present. The Kashmir conflict has defied solution until today, and due to this it bears comparison to the Israeli-Palestinian conflict. In this monograph, I discuss the politics of the conflict that is entrenched with many issues between the two neighbors. Presenting a historical view of the Indo-Pakistan wars and the crisis in Kashmir, I also try to present various explanations for the persistence of this conflict between India and Pakistan.

The monograph offers explanations of the mutual claims to the state of Kashmir; the lack of political will among political leaders of India and Pakistan; the Pakistan military's interest in keeping the conflict aflame in order to retain its dominance of Pakistan's politics, defense and foreign policies, even when the country is under civilian rule; and the hostile posture taken by Pakistan's elite society towards India. Although the army's current chief, General Bajwa, has taken a softer line towards India and the conflict between the two nation-states and appears to support dialogue with India, it may not be the case with other generals, especially since Pakistan's Inter-Services Intelligence (ISI) has become a state within a state. Unless the Pakistani military is depoliticized and sent back into barracks, achieving long-lasting peace with Pakistan may not be easy. Nonetheless, India should not give up trying. The monograph also discusses the ongoing Muslim insurgency, which erupted in the Kashmir Valley in late 1989 and continues today, although intermittently. This monograph examines its causes and the unsuccessful attempts undertaken by various Indian governments, including the current Modi government, to put it down. The same was pledged by the Nehru government.

Had the successive governments respected Kashmir's autonomy under Article 370 and not meddled with the domestic affairs of the state as they very often did, and in a heavy-handed manner, perhaps the Muslim insurgency would not have occurred and the Pakistan military would not have had the opportunity to manipulate and exploit the situation in the Valley to keep the insurgency afloat and use it to its advantage by damaging India's image in the community of nations because of its alleged human rights abuses.

I have tried to identify several alternative solutions to this problem in the monograph, and I suggest some solutions that the parties to the conflict could possibly accept to end this conflict. The monograph concludes by arguing that Modi, a Hindu nationalist, is in a good position to end this conflict, because he enjoys great credibility among a large segment of the Indian population. His party – the BJP – won a landslide victory in the 2014 parliamentary elections. Any concessions Modi may offer to the parties, especially Pakistan, in pursuit of achieving long-lasting peace, will be a decision that most Indians are likely to accept because he is first a Hindu nationalist and second a dedicated member of the Rashtriya Swayamsevek Sangh.

I hope that this work will be a small contribution to an understanding of this enduring conflict by readers, scholars and policy makers. Indians and Pakistanis lived together for more than four thousand years as one people sharing the same civilization, traditions, cultural mores, language, dress, food and more. But after the partition, India and Pakistan have become hostile powers possessing hundreds of nuclear warheads because of the Kashmir issue. As the former US President Bill Clinton once said, South Asia has become the world's most dangerous region due to this conflict. I, like most Indians, believe that peace can be achieved between India and Pakistan if the Indian and Pakistani elites can bury the hatchet and pursue peace with grit and determination in the interests of their peoples, so that Indians and Pakistanis can devote their energies, talents, skills and resources to addressing their myriad social, economic, educational, health and environmental problems and thus help transform their societies into prosperous ones. Indians are peace-loving and tolerant people and, as the polls indicate, they desire peace with Pakistan; therefore, it is incumbent on India's leaders to pursue peace with Pakistan. As my late philosophy colleague used to say, Hinduism is a religion which is intolerant of intolerance. This definition is contrary to what the RSS preaches when it advocates against other religious groups and Pakistan. Hinduism is not a religion of hate; it is no wonder that in India, so many religious denominations and sects, including Christianity (Christianity came to India in the first century before it went to Europe), have flourished.

I thank my colleagues Drs. Henry Sirgo and Muhammad Haque in the Department of Social Sciences and my wife Glory Karne profusely for encouraging me to proceed with this project at a time when I was not sure I had the energy and time to undertake this endeavor. I also want to thank Aakash Chakrabarty, my editor at Routledge, and Shloka Chauhan, the editorial assistant, for guiding me meticulously on citations and other aspects of the manuscript to help improve it.

India–Pakistan wars and the Kashmir crisis

Since the partition of British India into India and Pakistan in 1947, the Kashmir dispute between them has become an intractable conflict, defying solution. India and Pakistan have fought four wars over Kashmir, in 1947, 1965, 1971 (the Kashmir dispute was peripherally related) and 1999, and were engaged in a number of crises in the past. Currently, India and Pakistan are in another serious crisis with portents of another war. The Kashmir dispute has become an intractable problem, as both India and Pakistan claim the same territory as their own. So, the purpose of this book is first to briefly discuss the origins of the Kashmir dispute, the wars and crises, including the current crisis that has erupted between India and Pakistan; second, to discuss briefly the intermittent, unsuccessful initiatives taken by both India and Pakistan, as well as by others, to resolve the conflict; and finally, to offer explanations for the persistence of this festering conflict between India and Pakistan and suggest alternative solutions, including a viable one for consideration by the parties to resolve the conflict. We begin our discussion first with the origins of the Kashmir dispute, and the wars and the crises that have occurred between India and Pakistan.

The origins of the dispute and the First War (1947–49)

In 1947, when British India was partitioned into India and Pakistan, Hari Singh, the Hindu autocratic and unpopular maharaja (king) of Jammu and Kashmir (J&K), a predominantly Muslim state, resisted pressure to accede to either Pakistan or India, hoping to seek either independence or autonomy from both countries. To buy time and to accomplish this goal, Singh signed a standstill agreement with Pakistan on August 16. Meanwhile, communal rioting erupted in the neighboring state, Punjab, between Hindus/ Sikhs and the Muslims, as this state was divided between India and Pakistan. In September, the communal rioting in Punjab spilled into J&K. Muslims in the western part of Kashmir rebelled against King Hari Singh and established their independent (Azad) Kashmir government. So, to force the other part of state under Singh to accede to Pakistan, on October 22, 1947, the Pathan-armed tribes of the Northwest Frontier Province (NWFP, which is now called Khyber-Pakhtunkhwa) invaded Kashmir and pushed themselves fifteen miles from the state's capital city, Srinagar. Alarmed by this invasion, King Singh sought India's military assistance, but India refused to aid him unless he signed the instrument of accession to the country, a standard procedure under which princely states acceded to either India or Pakistan. Following Singh's signing of the Instrument of Accession on October 27,[1] and after receiving the consent of Sheikh Abdullah, the most popular leader and founder of the secular party, the National Conference (NC), the Indian armed forces entered Kashmir to repel the raiders on the same day. The local Muslims, mostly members of the NC Party, provided the logistical support for the Indian troops. This intervention by India infuriated Pakistani Governor-General Mohammed Ali Jinnah, the founding father of Pakistan. On the evening of October 27, Jinnah ordered Lt. General Sir Douglas Gracey, the chief of the Pakistan army, to dispatch Pakistan regular troops into Kashmir, but persuaded by Field Marshall Sir Claude Auchinleck, the supreme commander during the transition period, Jinnah withdrew his orders. However, in November, Jinnah sanctioned the transfer of military supplies to the invaders while also sending Pakistan regular troops to join their effort in early 1948 as "volunteers," though not admitting its direct involvement until July 1948. As the fighting continued, on January 1, 1948, on the advice of British Governor-General Lord Mountbatten, though opposed by his Deputy Prime Minister Sarder V. Patel, Prime Minister Jawaharlal Nehru lodged a complaint with the UN Security Council (UNSC) by invoking Articles 34 and 35 of the UN Charter (that call for Pacific Settlement of Disputes) against Pakistan, suspecting that it was behind the invasion.[2] In the complaint, as it had already been pledged by Lord Mountbatten in his letter addressed to Hari Singh on October 26, India reiterated its pledge of its conditional commitment to a "plebiscite or referendum under international auspices" once the aggressor was evicted – a pledge that India later regretted, as Pakistan insists on its implementation until to this day.

On January 20, 1948, the UNSC established a three-member UN Commission on India and Pakistan (UNCIP) to go to Kashmir, investigate the situation and exercise mediation. On April 21, the council expanded the commission to five and authorized it to restore peace and arrange for a plebiscite after the withdrawal of tribal troops from the part of J&K they occupied. But following Pakistani Foreign Minister Sir Mohammed Zafrullah Khan's admission on July 7, 1948, that his country's regular troops were in Kashmir, on August 13, the UNCIP passed a resolution calling on both India and Pakistan to conduct a plebiscite after they agreed to a ceasefire and after Pakistan's regular troops and tribesmen were completely withdrawn.[3] The ceasefire went into effect on January 1, 1949, while Pakistan was still in control of one-third of the J&K state, which was later called Azad (free) Kashmir or Pakistan-occupied Kashmir (POK), as India calls it. Again under the UNCIP resolution of August 13, 1948, the Observer Group in India and Pakistan (UNOGIP), the first ever by the UN, was sent to the region on January 24 to monitor the Ceasefire Line (CFL), which was later renamed as the Line of Control (LOC). The presence of the UNOGIP was approved by India and Pakistan following their agreement reached in Karachi on July 27, 1949. On January 5, 1949, the UNCIP reaffirmed the plebiscite. After that, Admiral Chester Nimitz, an American, was appointed by UN Secretary General Trygve Lie as plebiscite administrator, but he could not assume his functions, as India and Pakistan objected to his implementation by offering differing interpretations to the UNCIP resolutions on the issue of demilitarization of the state. So, in December 1949, the UNSC entrusted its President General A.G.L. McNaughton of Canada to negotiate a demilitarization plan in consultation with India and Pakistan. But it fell through, as Pakistan agreed only to simultaneous demilitarization while India chose to ignore it by raising the moral and legal aspects of the plan. On March 14, 1950, the UNSC passed another resolution affirming McNaughton's proposals and appointed the noted Australian judge, Sir Owen Dixon, as UN representative to replace the UNCIP. In September 1950, Dixon suggested a proposal limiting plebiscite only to the predominantly Muslim Kashmir Valley population, which both countries rejected. In April 1951, the UNSC appointed Dr. Frank Graham, the former US senator, as the UN representative. Between December 1951 and February 1953, Graham frantically tried to convince both India and Pakistan to accept the UNSC-supported demilitarization proposals with reduced military presence of both countries in Indian-administered Kashmir and Azad Kashmir (POK) preceding the conduct of a plebiscite, but to no avail, as both India and Pakistan rejected the proposal. Meanwhile, under temporary Article 370 of the Indian constitution, which came into effect in January 1950, the state of J&K was granted a special status of autonomy to have its own constitution, with no right for non-Kashmiris either to purchase land or settle in the state under Article 35A of 1954, which is, by the way, currently being challenged before India's Supreme Court.

Against the backdrop of this stalemate, Nehru and Pakistan Prime Minister Mohammad Ali Bogra met in June 1953 at the commonwealth conference in London and discussed the Kashmir issue. After that discussion, on August 20, 1953, both India and Pakistan temporarily agreed to take the issue out of the UN and resolve it directly. Subsequently, to the pleasant surprise of Pakistan, by the time Bogra visited New Delhi in 1953, as he had already notified Kashmir's new prime minister, Bakshi Ghulam Moham-mad, of his intention to conduct a plebiscite, Nehru told the same to the visiting Bogra in New Delhi, who returned to Pakistan triumphantly with Nehru's pledge. But Nehru's offer failed to take off due to Bogra's procras-tination, reportedly brought about by the conspiratorial politics of General Ayub Khan, who was plotting to seize power and who had needed hostility with India in order to realize goal-seizing power.

But following Pakistan's joining of the US-led Baghdad Pact in April 1954 and the South East Asian Treaty Organization (SEATO) in September 1956, Nehru reversed his position on the plebiscite, as he considered this decision by Pakistan as inimical to India's interests as a non-aligned state in the Cold War between the US-led bloc and the Soviet-led bloc. Nehru argued that because of Pakistan's alliance with the US, all agreements about the plebiscite in Kashmir became obsolete. Subsequently, in February 1954, the J&K state constituent assembly declared that Kashmir's accession to India was final. This position taken by the J&K state assembly was deemed by India as equivalent to a plebiscite, although the POK was not a party to this decision. India then told the UNSC that the issue of Kashmir was finally settled, notwithstanding that Pakistan and the UNSC had rejected that assertion. The UNSC met in January 1957 and reaffirmed its earlier resolutions on the plebiscite. In February 1957, the council authorized its president, Gunnar Jarring, to mediate between India and Pakistan on the proposals of demilitarization and plebiscite, but like his predecessors, Jar-ring, on his visit to the region, made no progress other than proposing to the UNSC in April that the issue be referred to arbitration, which Pakistan accepted, but India rejected. In September, as Pakistani Prime Minister Sir Feroz Khan Noon declared that his country was willing to withdraw its troops from Kashmir to meet India's preconditions, the UNSC once again sent Frank Graham to the area. He tried to secure an agreement between India and Pakistan but to no avail, as India again rejected his efforts. In March 1958, Graham submitted a report to the UNSC recommending that it arbitrate the dispute, but as usual, India rejected the proposal. From the mid-1950s onward, the Soviet Union rescued India with its frequent vetoes of the UNSC resolutions on Kashmir. Thereafter, the Kashmir issue practically died in the UNSC until it was raised again in 1963 and 1965.[4] Meanwhile, General Ayub Khan seized power through a military coup d'état in October 1958, which further hampered Indo-Pakistan relations. Having had been greatly attached to his ancestral J&K, Nehru took shifting positions on the Kashmir situation and died on May 27, 1964, without finding a solution. Lal Bahadur Shastri succeeded him as prime minister.

Meanwhile, during this ongoing dispute between India and Pakistan, the state of J&K underwent dramatic domestic political changes. For instance, in March 1948, King Singh handed over power to Sheikh Abdullah, who became prime minister of an interim government of the state. In 1949, the king abdicated the throne and his son Karan Singh succeed him as a regent, and under the temporary Article 370 of the Indian constitution, which, as noted earlier, came into effect in January 1950, the state was granted a special status by limiting the central government's powers over it to defense, communication and external affairs while disallowing non-Kashmiris to either settle in the state or buy property under Article 35A. But by 1953, Abdullah, who had supported the state's accession to India earlier, began to change his tune by calling for its independence. This stance by Abdullah resulted in his removal from power and arrest by Bakshi Ghulam Moham-mad, who by now had assumed the office of prime minister. In February 1954, the state constituent assembly, as noted earlier, affirmed the state's accession to India. Subsequently, under the seventh amendment to the Indian constitution, approved in 1956, the state, including the POK, became an integral part of India. This constitutional provision was approved by the J&K state constituent assembly in March 1957, and in December 1964, India announced that Articles 356 and 357 would also be applicable to the state of J&K, stating that under these articles, the state of J&K was brought under presidential rule (center's rule) as well as under Indian parliamentary legislation, thus whittling down the state's special status granted under Article 370 to the chagrin of the Kashmiris.[5]

As Kashmir's issue was deadlocked in the UN, persuaded by the Kennedy administration and the British government, India and Pakistan held five rounds of bilateral talks between December 1962 and April 1963 but failed to break the ice on the dispute. In October 1962, China inflicted a humiliating defeat on India to the glee of Pakistan. In March 1963, in the wake of India's protestation, Pakistan signed a border agreement with China ceding it some 2,050 square miles of the POK territory unilaterally. This agreement enabled China to build a road linking its Xinjiang province to Tibet. Pakistan and China subsequently became all-weather friends. By 1964, India rebuilt its military after its calamitous defeat by China on the assumption that India was not strong enough to respond to a Chinese attack. Meanwhile in 1965 tensions erupted between India and Pakistan that led to another war.

As a prelude to the September 1965 war, beginning in January 1965, Pakistan initiated a probing provocative action in the Rann of Kutch, a largely trackless wasteland and poorly demarcated border area in the Western Indian state of Gujarat, that led to several months of skirmishes between Indian and Pakistani troops. The skirmishes finally ended in May 1965 when, under Britain's mediation, the parties agreed to an international arbitration commission.[6] On the belief that India's tepid response during the skirmishes was a sign of its military weakness and that Pakistan was militarily strong vis-à-vis India, the country launched another war in September 1965.

The Second Kashmir War (September 1965)

Having been emboldened by a presumed victory against India in the Rann of Kutch, in May 1965, Pakistan made plans for "Operation Gibraltar" to recover Kashmir. As it did in 1947, it first sent Pakistani guerrillas into the Valley in August 1965, hoping that the Kashmiri Muslims would rise in rebellion against India. Instead, the Kashmiris apprehended the Pakistanis and handed them over to the Indian authorities. But when Indian troops crossed the Indo-Pakistan international border, Pakistan launched an attack on Jammu on September 1. In response, India launched a series of attacks across Pakistan's province of Punjab towards the cities of Lahore and Sialkot and battled the Pakistani army. As the clashes continued, and as they reached a stalemate with each side occupying some portions the other's territory, the UNSC, supported by the United States, Britain and the USSR, called for an immediate ceasefire, which India and Pakistan accepted and which came into effect on September 23.[7] Although the war was brief, it was a bitter one. Neither country could claim to be a decisive winner in this war. In January 1966, at the invitation of Soviet Premier Alexei Kosygin, both Shastri and Ayub Khan met in the city of Tashkent (Republic of Uzbekistan); their meeting is known as the Tashkent Declaration. On January 10, the agreement was formalized and the hostilities ended followed by the withdrawal of Indian and Pakistani forces to their pre-war ceasefire lines. Under this agreement, both countries agreed to not resort to force and to resolve the Kashmir dispute peacefully, to not interfere in each other's internal affairs, and to renew diplomatic relations between the two countries.[8] Shastri died of a heart attack in Tashkent right after he had signed the Declaration, and Nehru's daughter, Indira Gandhi, succeeded Shastri as prime minister. Meanwhile, in March 1969, Ayub Khan resigned and General Agha Muhammad Yahya Khan succeeded him as president. In 1971, India and Pakistan fought a third war, this time over Bangladesh's independence, in which the Kashmir dispute was peripherally involved.

The Third Indo-Pakistan War (December 1971)

As West Pakistani leader of the Pakistan Peoples Party (PPP), Zulfiqar Ali Bhutto failed to reach a power-sharing agreement with East Pakistani leader Sheikh Mujib Rahman of the Awami League Party, who had won a majority of seats to the parliament in the December 1970 election. Mujib was denied the post to be the prime minister of Pakistan. As a consequence, the East Bengalis (Bangladeshis) launched a rebellious movement seeking independence from West Pakistan. General Yahya Khan ordered a crackdown of the rebellion, resulting in the fleeing of nearly ten million East Bengalis into India. India supported the Bangladeshi guerrillas known as *Mukti Bahini* (freedom brothers) by providing them with aid and sanctuary in the neighboring West Bengal state of India. Indira Gandhi approached the Nixon administration to intervene and persuade General Yahya Khan to end the crackdown so that the refugees could return back to East Pakistan. But Nixon did not intervene, as Yahya Khan as its US ally played a diplomatic role in being a conduit to US opening to China. So, on December 3, 1970, Pakistan launched both ground and air attacks on India's western front – the states of Kashmir, Punjab and Rajasthan. This attack drew India formally into war and Indian troops moved on all fronts – west and east – against Pakistan, and on December 6, India granted formal recognition of Bangladesh as an independent country. In a swift military operation, the Indian army moved toward the city of Dacca, Bangladesh, and moved in on the Pakistani military. On December 17, the troops entered the city and accepted the Pakistani troops' surrender. Immediately thereafter, India declared a unilateral ceasefire on the western front after it made some gains along the ceasefire lines in Kashmir while losing some territory to Pakistan in the Chamb sector of Kashmir. Pakistan readily reciprocated to India's declaration. Thereafter, General Yahya Khan resigned on December 20, and Bhutto succeeded him first as president, and later as prime minister. In this war, the Pakistani troops, in their crackdown, killed nearly two million Bangladeshis.[9]

On July 2, 1972, Gandhi signed the Simla agreement with Bhutto in India. Under this agreement, both India and Pakistan committed themselves to "settling their differences through bilateral negotiations or by any other peaceful means mutually agreed upon between them," and that the "basic issues and causes which bedeviled the relations between the two countries for the last 25 years shall be resolved by peaceful means." They also agreed that in "Jammu and Kashmir, the Line of Control (LOC) resulting from the cease-fire of December 17, 1971, shall be respected by both sides without prejudice to the recognized position of either side."[10] Henceforth, in resolving the Kashmir dispute, this agreement shifted responsibility from the UN to bilateral negotiations and subsequently led to the renewal of diplomatic relations between the two countries. On July 24, 1973, they both signed another agreement in New Delhi, agreeing to repatriate nearly 90,000 plus Pakistani prisoners of war, except for 195 who were held to be tried for crimes against humanity but subsequently released without a trial. It is ironic that while Pakistan demanded that India agree to a plebiscite in the Indian-administered J&K, in 1974, it unilaterally detached the Gilgit Agency and Baltistan from the Azad Kashmir and made them part of Pakistan by ignoring the UN Security Council's longstanding resolutions, as India had done of J&K when it had integrated Kashmir into its union in 1956, however, with the consent of the state constituent assembly resolution. As hopeful signs of resolving the dispute peacefully persisted under Bhutto's leadership, in July 1977, Lt. Gen. Zia ul Haq, the chief of army, ousted him from power in a military coup and ruled Pakistan as a military dictator until his mysterious death in September 1988 in a plane crash. Zia had Bhutto executed under some trumped-up charges in 1979, and transformed Pakistan from a religiously moderate state into an Islamist state. Today, Pakistan is paying a heavy price for what Zia did in terms of the rise of Islamic fanaticism and sectarianism. During General Zia's regime, Indo-Pakistani relations became frozen and the Kashmir issue took a backstage seat.

Meanwhile, the state of J&K witnessed a dramatic political change in that Sheikh Abdullah, who had all along insisted on a plebiscite in the past, in July 1972, dropped that demand, and on January 12, 1975, he signed an accord with Indira Gandhi's government, under which the state would enjoy a special status under Article 370 but as an integral part of India. In February 1975, Abdullah became the state's chief minister, and he remained in that post until his death in September 1982. By accepting the state as an integral part of India, Abdullah, a very popular leader at that time, had undercut Pakistan's demand for self-determination. He was succeeded by his son Dr. Farooq Abdullah, who took a similar stance on the state's integration with India, however with undiluted autonomy for the state.[11] Meanwhile, following Gandhi's assassination by her Sikh security guards in 1984, her son Rajiv Gandhi succeeded her as prime minister.

The Kashmiri Muslim separatist insurgency and the 1990 Indo-Pak crisis

In the March 1987 legislative assembly elections, the opposition party, known as the Muslim United Front (MUF), a party of disparate groups, had expected to do well, but won only five out of the state's seventy-six seats, while the NC-Congress coalition won sixty-six seats. The MUF attributed this legislative victory to Prime Minister Rajiv Gandhi's fraudulent rigging of the elections. Having been alienated and angered in the belief that the center was meddling in the state's domestic political affairs, the Kashmiri youth, mostly the college educated, launched an indigenous insurgency in December 1989, demanding self-determination for the state. Immediately, Pakistan's Inter-Services Intelligence seized the opportunity to support the insurgents with funds, as well as training in POK. The Kashmir insurgency movement synchronized with V. P. Singh assuming the office of prime minister in December 1989.

The insurgency movement consisted of three principal umbrella groups. One group was composed of Muslim fundamentalists who were pro-Pakistan with links to the fundamentalist Pakistan party Jamaat-i-Islami; the second umbrella group was tied to the Jammu and Kashmir Liberation Front (JKLF) established in 1965 and demanded an independent Kashmir, and the third group was the Jammu and Kashmir Peoples' League (JKPL), which had a pro-Pakistani orientation. These groups demanded a plebiscite as had been pledged by India and guaranteed by the UN Resolutions of 1948–49 so that the Kashmiris would have the right of self-determination, a demand supported by Pakistan. As the uprising gathered force, the state plunged into anarchy. This deteriorating situation prompted Singh's government to dismiss Chief Minister Abdullah in January 1990 and bring it under president's rule by appointing Jagmohan Malhotra as the state's governor. Malhotra adopted highhanded repressive tactics to put down the insurgency on the belief that it was instigated by Pakistan.[12] As the result of Malhotra's scorched earth policy against the insurgents, Singh and Benazir Bhutto, who had assumed the office of prime minister in 1988, began to engage in a war of words. As Dr. Summit Ganguly describes, Bhutto publicly called for the liberation of Kashmir and talked about fighting a thousand year war against India. In response, Singh commented that it remains to be seen if Pakistan could last a thousand hours in a war with India. As the troops of both countries moved towards the front lines, amidst these rising tensions, India's foreign ministers of India and Pakistan, Inder Kumar Gujral and Sahabzada Yaqub Khan, respectively, met in New York and agreed to exercise restraint in both words and actions while stating their positions on the Kashmir dispute. As tensions continued to mount, fearing another war between India and Pakistan including the potential use of nuclear weapons this time, the Bush Administration's Deputy National Security Advisor Robert Gates visited both New Delhi and Islamabad and helped to avert a war between the two countries.[13] In May 1990, Malhotra was succeeded by Girish Saxena (May 1990–93 and 1998–2003), who was equally repressive in his attempts to crush the rebellion. Meanwhile, the Indian government sent increasing numbers of military and paramilitary forces numbering more than 300,000 to help put down the militancy. It dismissed Abdullah's government in August 1990 and brought the state under central rule. And under July 1990's Jammu and Kashmir Disturbed Areas Act and 1958's Armed Forces Special Powers Act (AFSPA) as the backdrop, the security forces allegedly committed a series of human rights abuses according to the Amnesty International, Human Rights Watch, and the US Department annual reports. The abuses, among others, included mock encounters and inhuman treatment of prisoners and suspects with beatings, burning with cigarettes, suspension, torture and rape. India, as a democratic state, tarnished its image by these practices. The Muslim militants were equally brutal with a difference only in degree towards the Kashmiri Pandits, who had accounted for 3% of the pre-insurgency Kashmir Valley population. Among other atrocities, the militants committed barbaric killings, kidnappings, gang rapes, lootings and arson and engaged in terrorizing campaigns. These atrocities led to a mass exodus of more than 260,000 Pandits as refugees to other cities of India, including Jammu, which is predominantly Hindu. The militants were engaged in an ethnic cleansing to free the Valley of Hindus.[14]

By early 1996, the central government adopted a multi-pronged approach to deal with the insurgency. For example, on one hand, it lifted presidential rule and let Farooq take charge of the state as chief minister after his party had won a landslide victory in the September state legislative assembly elections. The disparate thirty-party coalition, known as the All Parties Hurriyat (Freedom) Conference (APHC), denounced and boycotted the elections. On the other hand, the center promoted several pro-Indian Muslim counterinsurgency groups to fight the insurgents along with its security forces. In February 1996, it also released from jail four pro-Pakistani separatist leaders – Imran Rahi of the Hizbul-Mujahideen (HUM), Bilal Lodhi of Al-Barq, Babbar Badr of the Muslim Janbaz Force (MJF) and Ghulam Mohiuddin Lone of the Muslim Mujahideen (MM) – and initiated talks with them. They agreed to talks with the government with no preconditions attached and without Pakistan being involved. But the APHC denounced them for agreeing to talk to the Indian government without Pakistan's inclusion and advocated for their expulsion from their organizations. Meanwhile, inter-group clashes began to erupt, thus undermining their cause. For example, in 1995 alone, 167 clashes took place among them, and as a result, 107 militants were killed. Even group leaders were targeted for murder, including Syed Ali Shah Geelani of the Jamaat-i-Islami and Abdul Ghani Lone of the People's Conference, who are pro-Pakistan. In addition, many Kashmiris were not only tired of the long violence and bloodshed, but were also disenchanted with the ostentatious lifestyle of leaders such as Geelani and Abdul Ghani Bhat of the Muslim Conference, who came under increasing public criticism and whose commitment to the cause was questioned as they began to enrich themselves with foreign money.[15]

In light of the above-mentioned approach taken by the Indian government and the positive response it received from some of the militant leaders, it appeared that the center had gained control of the Muslim militancy problem. But given the Farooq government's inept rule and its failure to address the pressing socio-economic problems of the Kashmiris, and Pakistan's continued active role in fostering and promoting its home-based mercenary outfits to fight in Kashmir, peace became elusive, and since 1997, the insurgency was again revived and intensified. Motivated by a desire to incite sectarian violence, the militants began to kill scores of innocent Hindus and Sikhs indiscriminately, especially beginning in 1998. In the context of this Kashmir ongoing insurgency, Indo-Pakistan relations witnessed ebb and flow. For example, while Indo-Pak relations deteriorated during the two unfinished five-year terms of Prime Minister Bhutto (1988–90 and 1993–96), who was removed at the behest of the military, they began to witness a thaw in the unfinished five-year terms of Nawaz Sharif (1990–93, and 1997–99), who was also removed at the dictates of the military.

A temporary thaw in Indo-Pak relations (1997–99)

Nawaz Sharif took office as prime minister in February 1997. Under his leadership. Indo-Pakistan relations witnessed a thaw, though temporarily. For example, in March, dialogue at the foreign secretary level was resumed. In April, Pakistani Foreign Minister Gohar Ayub Khan met India's prime minister, I. K. Gujral, at a meeting of the Non-Aligned Movement (NAM) held in New Delhi to break the ice. In May of the same year, the two prime ministers met at the South Asian Association of Regional Cooperation (SAARC) summit held at Male, The Maldives, and agreed not only to resume talks at the foreign secretary level but also to form eight joint "working groups" which would also include, for the first time since 1972, the Kashmir issue. Subsequently, by September, foreign secretaries held three meetings in spite of artillery exchanges at a number of points along the LOC. In September, both prime ministers again met in New York on the sidelines of the UN General Assembly session.[16] Meanwhile, in the March 1998 parliamentary elections, the BJP-dominated United Front coalition won, and the government led by Prime Minister Atal Behari Vajpayee took a harsher stance against Pakistan. For instance, its Home Minister L. K. Advani threatened to pursue the terrorists by going into Pakistan-occupied Kashmir. Indo-Pakistani tensions became further aggravated following their nuclear testing in May 1998, causing concerns in the international community that the Kashmir conflict might become a catalyst for war between two countries with potential use of nuclear weapons. Both countries came under severe condemnation by the international community. The UNSC, recognizing that Kashmir was "the root cause of tensions between the two countries," advised India and Pakistan to avoid "threatening military movements, cross-border violations, or other provocative acts" and urged them to "discuss all outstanding problems including Kashmir."[17] The nuclear testing raised tempers so high between India and

Pakistan that on July 29, when Vajpayee and Sharif met at the tenth summit of the SAARC held in Colombo, Sri Lanka, Sharif insisted that no progress was possible between the two countries unless the "core issue" of Kashmir was resolved. He characterized the meeting with Vajpayee as "zero" and warned that India's "intransigence" was pushing the region to the brink of war. India's foreign secretary, K. Raghunath, responded by terming Pakistan's obsessive focus on the single issue of Kashmir as "neurotic" and that serious dialogue should not be used to "pursue a limited agenda or promote a propagandist exercise." The meeting coincided with firing at the LOC in Kashmir in which 30 villagers were killed, leading to large-scale evacuation from the border areas.[18] But when the prime ministers met on September 23 for the second time, on the sidelines of the UN General Assembly session in New York, there was a dramatic change in the tenor of their encounter. It was friendly, and both agreed to resolve the Kashmir issue "peacefully" and sought to focus on trade and people-to-people contacts. Subsequently, India agreed to buy sugar and powder from Pakistan, and after a decade of lacuna of no games between the two countries, Pakistan's cricket team visited India and played cricket in November 1998. In February 1999, Pakistan permitted India to run buses from New Delhi to Lahore. In February 1999, on Sharif's invitation, Vajpayee visited Lahore (commonly known as "bus diplomacy") and, at the end of their summit, the leaders issued the Lahore Declaration in which they agreed to engage in consultations on security matters, including nuclear doctrines, initiate confidence-building measures in both nuclear and conventional areas, and establish appropriate communications mechanisms to help diminish the possibility of nuclear war by accident or misinterpretation. They also agreed to continue their respective moratoriums on further nuclear tests unless their "supreme national interest" was in jeopardy.[19] However, this declaration did not sit well with elements of the military, which also included the future dictator General Pervez Musharraf. It was no wonder that in May–July 1999, the military provoked a mini-war, called the Kargil War, within Indian-administered Kashmir, presumably to undercut the improving relations between India and Pakistan.

The Kargil War of 1999 and its resolution

In May 1999, nearly 1,500 Pakistan-backed Muslim militants known as the Islamic Mujahideen (Islamic Freedom Fighters) infiltrated six miles into the Kargil region of North Kashmir by crossing the LOC. The militants, who were mostly Afghani, were joined by the Pakistani regulars and occupied nearly thirty-five well-fortified positions located at 16,000 and 18,000 feet above sea level atop the most inhospitable frigidly cold ridges in the Great Himalayan range facing Dras, Kargil, Batalik and the Mushko Valley sectors stretching over 30 miles. Beginning on May 26, following a detection by the Indian army patrols during May 8–15, India launched air attacks known as Operation Vijay (victory) against the bunkers from which the intruders had been firing upon the Indian troops below the ridges. As the battle raged on between May 31 and June 11, the Indian troops cleared up some pockets of resistance and cut off the supply lines to the intruders by outflanking them in the Jubar Heights. And as early as June 6, the Indian troops also launched a major offensive in the Kargil and Dras sectors accompanied by air strikes in order to protect the only highway linking Srinagar to the city of Leh in the Ladakh region from the Pakistani threat. Meanwhile, on June 10, Pakistan returned seven mutilated bodies of soldiers to New Delhi, outraging India. In the face of India's fury, on June 12, Pakistan's Foreign Minister Sartaj Aziz visited New Delhi to talk to Foreign Minister Jaswant Singh. But talks failed as India called Pakistan an aggressor for violating the LOC, while Aziz, questioning the validity of the line, called for a joint working group to help settle India's claim of the Kargil, which Singh angrily rejected.

As the battle turned bloodier, the Clinton administration intervened to help defuse the crisis. For instance, in the second week of June, Bruce Riedel, Special Assistant to President Clinton, in a briefing at Foreign Press Center, asserted the inviolability of the LOC. He stated that the president, in his recent letter to both prime ministers, had stressed that point. And on June 15, in separate telephone conversations, Clinton told Sharif to withdraw the infiltrators from across the LOC and that he appreciated Vajpayee for displaying restraint in the conflict. To Pakistan's further sense of isolation, the G-8, at their annual meeting in Cologne, Germany, June 19–20, came out strongly in support of India's contention that the Kargil crisis was precipitated by mercenaries backed by Pakistani troops. In a communique issued on June 20, the G-8, in unequivocal terms, condemned the violation of the LOC and dubbed Pakistan's military action as "irresponsible" in trying to change the status quo at the LOC and called on it to end the intrusion. The communique also urged the two countries to resolve the Kashmir dispute through "dialogue." This position was also supported by China. The G-8 statement was later followed by a visit to Islamabad by a delegation led by General Anthony Zinni, Commander-in-Chief of the US Central Command. On behalf of President Clinton, General Zinni again asked Sharif to withdraw troops from across the LOC. A day after Zinni's visit on June 28, Sharif rushed to Beijing seeking Chinese diplomatic support for the conflict. But the Chinese told him that he could not count on their support, so he cut short his six-day visit and returned home disappointed. Meanwhile, on June 20, Indian troops, after a fierce battle with a loss of fifty lives, recaptured Tololing Hill in the Dras sector, and on July 4, they recaptured Tiger Hill, which is considered to be the most strategic point in the Dras sector, as it overlooks the Srinagar-Leh Highway. As the Indian troops steadily recaptured one hill or ridge after another and as Pakistan's isolation in the world community increased (only Saudi Arabia and United Arab Emirates supported Pakistan), it desperately sought a face-saving formula to extricate itself from its miscalculated adventure. So, on July 3, Sharif requested a meeting with Clinton on "an urgent basis" and met with him on July 4 in Washington. After a three-hour meeting, both leaders issued a joint statement in which Sharif agreed to withdraw the intruders. The statement indicated that the forces that are across the LOC need to be returned to the Pakistani side. This was followed by the White House statement which said, among other things, that the president shared with Sharif the view that the current fighting "contains the seeds of wider conflict" and that "it was vital for the peace of South Asia that the LOC in Kashmir be respected by both parties in accordance with their 1972 Simla accord," and that "bilateral dialogue which begun in Lahore in February provided the best for resolving all issues dividing India and Pakistan, including Kashmir," and that the president would take "personal interest in encouraging an expeditious resumption and intensification of those bilateral efforts once the sanctity of the LOC has been fully restored." As the meeting with Sharif progressed, Clinton took frequent intervals to call on Vajpayee in order to "keep him fully appraised of the discussion," as he had declined the invitation to go to Washington. Following Sharif's agreement with Clinton, beginning July 11, the infiltrators began retreating from Kargil, as India set July 16 as a deadline for the total withdrawal. On July 12, in an address to the nation, the beleaguered Sharif defended his July 4 agreement with Clinton as well as his request to the intruders to withdraw from the Indian territory. He also defended his Kargil policy as something presumably designed to draw the attention of the international community to the Kashmir issue, although he later accused General Musharraf of having had been the architect of the war adventure. In this war, more than 400 Indian soldiers, 679 intruders and 30 Pakistani regulars were killed, and more were wounded.[20] Sharif's agreement to withdraw the intruders had upset the military so much that on October 12, it ousted him from power in a bloodless coup and General Pervez Musharraf assumed power first as chief executive and later as president by holding a so-called referendum. Sharif was tried by the Anti-Terrorist Court on charges of treason and criminal conspiracy and sentenced to death. He was subsequently exiled to Saudi Arabia.[21]

The intensification of the Kashmir insurgency and tense relations with the Musharraf regime (1999–2003)

As the coup had upset India, it got Pakistan suspended from the Common-wealth Conference, and tensions rose again between India and Pakistan. The artillery firings across the LOC were once again intensified, and on December 24, a New Delhi-bound plane carrying 178 passengers from Kathmandu, Nepal, was hijacked by the Pakistan-based Harkat ul-Mujahideen (HUM) terrorists and forced to land in Kandahar, Afghanistan. The hijackers demanded release of thirty-five Kashmiri militants, including the Pakistani cleric Maulana Masood Azhar jailed in India, in exchange for the passengers. When India's government refused to concede to their demands, they killed an Indian man who was on a honeymoon with his wife. Pressured by the passengers' relatives, on December 31, India exchanged them with the release of three hardcore militants, including Azhar. This episode was a humiliation to India's image. India implicated Pakistan in the hijacking and lobbied the Clinton administration to declare it a "terrorist state," but to no avail. Unlike his predecessors, Musharraf came out openly in support of terrorists by declaring, "Islam does not recognize political boundaries, and Jihad is a concept of God."[22]

Emboldened by the successful results of their hijacking, militants escalated their assaults and suicide bombings against innocent bystanders and the security forces in Kashmir. Realizing that negotiations with militants and the APHC leaders were essential to resolve this conflict, in November 2000, on the eve of the beginning of Ramadan, the Vajpayee government declared a unilateral ceasefire and invited them for talks. It also agreed to talk to Pakistan if the latter ceased supporting the cross-border terrorism. The APHC leaders, including its chairman at that time, Abdul Ghani Bhat, welcomed it. The Musharraf government agreed to abide by the cease-fire declaration along the LOC. However, some of the Pakistani-based militant groups such as the Lashkar-e-Taiba (TEB), Hizb-ul-Mujahideen (HUM), Jaish-e-Mohammed (JEM) – founded by Maulana Azhar after he was released by India from the hijacked plane), and Al-Umar-Mujahideen (AUM) rejected the ceasefire, declaring it a sham and vowing to liberate Kashmir through Jihad against pagan India. They escalated terrorism not only in Kashmir, but also took it to places like India's capital, New Delhi, and other cities on the belief that they would go to Paradise directly when they died as martyrs fighting pagan India. Quite a few of the terrorist outfits also included non-Kashmiri groups who were funded and promoted by the Pakistani military.[23] Hoping to persuade the APHC leaders to talk to his government, on April 5, 2001, Vajpayee appointed a noted politician and former Congress cabinet minister K. C. Pant as his interlocutor. Pant extended an invitation not only to the APHC leaders but also to other politicians from Kashmir who were committed to a peaceful resolution of the conflict. But the APHC leaders rejected the invitation on the ground that Pakistan was not included for talks. But as India's unilateral ceasefire declaration only helped the militants to escalate their terrorism, and as the APHC leaders refused to participate in the talks, Pant's efforts failed.[24] Thereafter, the Vajpayee government ended the six-month ceasefire and invited Pakistani dictator Musharraf for talks without conditions on the Kashmir conflict. Musharraf accepted the invitation, and the summit talks were held at Agra, near New Delhi, on July 14–16, 2001. They failed, however, as Musharraf insisted that Kashmir was the "core issue" to be addressed, while Vajpayee focused on Pakistan's need to end its support for the Kashmiri insurgency, as well as on resolution of other bilateral issues such as drug trafficking, Sir Creek and the Wular Barrage.[25] Although both leaders had agreed to meet again at the forthcoming November UN General Assembly meeting, they did not meet, as India became furious over a JEM-led suicide bomb attack of the J&K state assembly building on October 1, 2001, in which thirty-eight innocent civilians were killed. This was followed by another deadly attack on the Indian parliament building on December 13 by members of the Lashkar-e-Toiba (LET), in which forty people including five terrorists were killed as the parliament was in session. In response to these attacks, to compel the Musharraf regime to stop its support for the cross-border attacks, the Vajpayee government took a series of retaliatory measures, which included cutting off of road and rail links to Pakistan; banning of India's airspace for Pakistan commercial flights; recalling of India's ambassador to Islamabad, and deployment of nearly 800,000 Indian troops along the LOC. Alarmed by the potential threat of another Indo-Pakistan war, the Bush administration pressured the Musharraf regime to break its ties with the Jihadists. Musharraf pledged that he would not let his soil be used for cross-border terrorism, but he still allowed it. This was evidenced by the May 14, 2002, LET-led attack on army quarters at Kaluchak on the outskirts of Jammu, in which thirty people were killed and forty-eight wounded, most being children and their mothers. This crime infuriated Vajpayee so greatly that he visited the soldiers along the frontiers in Kashmir and asked them to prepare for a "decisive battle" to end terrorism. On May 27, Musharraf responded by warning India that if "war was thrust upon us we will respond with full might." In the wake of these rising tensions, Bush administration officials visited both India and Pakistan and helped to defuse the tensions by extracting a pledge from Musharraf that he would stop cross-border terrorism and would shut down the terrorist training camps.[26] Subsequently, although the Vajpayee government insisted that it would not engage in dialogue with Pakistan until the latter completely stopped cross-border terrorism, as a gesture of goodwill it lifted the ban on Pakistan commercial airlines and withdrew its naval ships back to the port of Mumbai and its troops from the borders. Meanwhile, in October 2002, the Vajpayee government conducted fair and open elections to the J&K state assembly, in which the People's Democratic Party (PDP) led by Mufti Mohammed Sayeed in coalition with the Congress Party, won a majority and formed government with Sayeed as chief minister. Sayeed adopted a policy of "healing touch" towards the militants by calling on the central government to release them from prison if they disavowed violence. Even though terrorism continued, on April 18, 2003, on a visit to Srinagar, Kashmir, Vajpayee at a public rally extended a "hand of friendship" to Pakistan, calling for dialogue and reconciliation. In response, on April 28, the prime minister at that time, Zafarullah Jamali, called Vajpayee and invited him to visit Islamabad. On May 2, Vajpayee told the parliament that he would like to start a "decisive and conclusive dialogue" with Pakistan to end the decades of hostility between the two countries. And on November 22, on the day of Eid, Jamali declared a unilateral ceasefire, which India welcomed, and guns fell silent along the LOC. On January 6, 2004, Vajpayee and Musharraf, while attending the meeting of the SARC held in Islamabad, met on the sidelines of the summit and issued a historic joint statement, in which Musharraf pledged to end cross-border terrorism in exchange for Vajpayee's agreement to start talks on Kashmir.[27]

Composite dialogue launched, but fails (2004–14)

The Congress-led coalition (United Progressive Alliance-UPA) under Prime Minister Manmohan Singh, which succeeded the Vajpayee government in May 2004, launched composite dialogue with the Musharraf regime to resolve eight issues: Siachen, Sir Creek, Wullar barrage project, terrorism, economic cooperation and Kashmir. Immediately thereafter, joint working groups began meeting in India and Pakistan regularly to address these issues. As part of the confidence-building measures, both countries launched people-to-people contacts and decided to open a bus route from Srinagar to Muzaffarabad (POK) and another bus link between Sindh and Rajasthan. On April 17, 2005, as part of cricket diplomacy, Musharraf visited New Delhi to witness a game between India and Pakistan. General Musharraf later held talks with Singh, and they both issued a joint statement agreeing to have normal trade and political relations and to proceed with the peace process between the two countries. They also agreed to open two more trade routes between Srinagar and Muzaffarabad and between Poonch and Rawalakot (POK). Despite this ongoing composite dialogue, terrorism continued, this time spreading beyond J&K. For example, on October 29,

2005, on the eve of Diwali (festival of lights), three blasts ripped through crowded markets in Delhi, killing 69 and wounding more than 200. Later on, terrorists struck in the cities of Varanasi, Bangalore and Hyderabad, killing dozens and wounding hundreds of people in each of these cities. And on July 11, 2006, terrorists again struck passenger trains in the city of Mumbai, killing 200 and wounding more than 700. Immediately thereafter, General Musharraf offered his condolences and pledged his cooperation in catching the culprits as India suspended the dialogue. The dialogue was renewed after Singh and Musharraf had agreed to create an anti-terror institutional mechanism on September 16, 2006, while they met on the sidelines at the summit of the non-aligned nations in Havana, Cuba. On December 6, 2006, in an interview with NDTV (India), Musharraf, among others, suggested a proposal such as the demilitarization of Kashmir, self-rule in both Kashmir states and their joint management to resolve the Kashmir imbroglio. Singh, while he welcomed Musharraf's proposal on the issues of demilitarization and self-rule, was ambivalent on joint management of Kashmir states.[28] Given the complexity of the Kashmir dispute and fearing that an open round of talks might not bear fruit, as Steve Coll notes, Tariq Aziz and Satinder Lambah of Pakistan and India, respectively, were authorized by their leaders to engage in parallel back channel talks on Kashmir and other issues, which began in 2004 and continued until 2007.[29] But, both the open and secret talks failed to bear fruit on many of the issues covered in the composite dialogue, given their complexity and the mutual mistrust pervading in both countries, cross-border terrorism albeit at reduced levels. Meanwhile, Musharraf began to encounter internal challenges to his rule from his opponents beginning in 2007 to the end of his regime in 2008, eventually forcing him to hold elections and transfer power to a democratically elected leadership.

In March 2008, democracy was restored when the PPP-led coalition government headed by Yousuf Raza Gilani became prime minister. And following Musharraf's resignation, Asif Ali Zardari (husband of Benazir Bhutto, who was assassinated on December 26, 2007) was elected president in September 2008. India welcomed the restoration of democracy and expressed the hope of continuing the composite dialogue with the new leadership to resolve its conflict. However, Gilani took an uncompromising stance on Kashmir, as he was opposed to what was proposed by Musharraf on the Kashmir issue. For example, on May 1, in an address to a joint session of the POK state legislature in Muzaffarabad, Gilani assured the members that there would be no compromise on Kashmir and that his government was seeking "result-oriented" talks with India. And on May 11, he dismissed Musharraf's proposals on Kashmir as "half-baked." In October

2008, on a visit to the LOC, the new army chief General Ashfaq Parvez Kayani pushed for a "national consensus" on Kashmir and reaffirmed the army's commitment to the Kashmir issue. Meanwhile, for the first time since the September 2003 ceasefire agreement, in late July 2008 border skirmishes flared up, in which four Pakistani soldiers and one Indian soldier were killed. On July 13, a suicide bomber attacked the Indian embassy in Kabul, Afghanistan, in which sixty Afghans and four Indian diplomats were killed. India and then Afghan President Hamid Karzai implicated Pakistan's ISI. While attending the UN General Assembly session in New York on September 24, Zardari met with Singh and renewed Pakistan's pledge of cooperation in fighting terrorism and holding a fifth round of talks. Zardari called the Kashmir militants "terrorists" for the first time, while all other Pakistani leaders call them "freedom fighters." In November 2008, Zardari was rebuked by the army chief Kayani for disavowing Pakistan's longstanding nuclear "first strike" policy against India. Despite contradictory positions taken by Pakistani leadership, the composite dialogue talks continued until December 2008.[30] The composite dialogue came to a sudden halt when ten Pakistani terrorists who, after arriving in Mumbai on November 26, committed a series of heinous terror attacks on a commuter train passenger terminus, the Oberoi Trident hotel complex, Taj Mahal Palace, the Cama children's hospital, the Jewish Center in the Nariman House and the Leopold Café, killing 171 people, including 6 Americans, 3 Britons and a Jewish couple, and wounding 150 people. In their security operation, the Indian elite national security guards battled the terrorists, killed nine of them and captured one alive (Mohammad Ajmal Amir Kasab) on November 29, after four days of mayhem. Ajmal Kasab confessed to his interrogators that he and his group were from Pakistan and that they were trained by Pakistani army men under the patronage of the LET headed by Hafiz Mohammad Saeed. Following this dastardly attack, India declared a "pause" on restarting dialogue and demanded that Pakistan return twenty to forty alleged terrorists to India for trial. Meanwhile, in December, the UNSC imposed sanctions on four leaders belonging to the LET and JEM. Pressured by the international community, the Bush administration and India's coercive diplomacy, the Gilani government appointed the Federal Investigation Agency (FIA) and arrested six of the eight ringleaders of the attack, including Zaki-ur-Rehman, Zarar Shaw, Hamd Amin Sadiq and Javed Iqbal.[31] They were subsequently tried off and on by frequently changed trial judges and trial lawyers and were finally released on the grounds of alleged lack of sufficient evidence, even though India had submitted to Pakistan massive amounts of incontrovertible evidence. India feared the Pakistani military would not allow the trial and conviction of the conspirators of the attack lest the terrorist leaders should implicate the ISI in the well-planned and a well-orchestrated Mumbai attack. So far, to India's incredulity, neither the Gilani government nor its successor Sharif government acknowledged that the terrorists came from Pakistan.

Despite a snail-speed investigation by the Gilani government, six months after the Mumbai attack, Singh and Zardari met on June 17, 2009, at the summit of the Shanghai Cooperation organization (SOG) held in Yekaterinburg, Russia, and agreed to renew talks at the foreign secretary level. Again, on July 17, Singh and Gilani met at the meeting of the non-aligned nations held at Sharm El Sheikh, Egypt, and issued a joint statement agreeing to renew the composite dialogue by delinking talks from the issue of terrorism. However, on September 29, 2009, when then Foreign Minister S. M. Krishna met his Pakistani counterpart Shah Mahmood Qureshi, Krishna reminded the latter that a broad-based dialogue hinged on Pakistan's prosecution of all those who were involved in the Mumbai attack. In April 2010, on the sidelines of the summit of the SAARC held in Thimphu, Bhutan, Singh and Gilani met and mandated their foreign secretaries to hold discussions on the modalities of restoring trust and confidence in order to pave the way for holding the composite dialogue. The dialogue took off the ground beginning in March 2011, as the Gilani government had pledged to investigate the Mumbai attack. In November 2011, attending the 17th SAARC summit held in the Maldives, Singh and Gilani met on the sidelines and expressed satisfaction at the progress made by the resumed dialogue talks and agreed to continue with the process with the aim of building a mutually productive relationship. On a private visit to the Sufi shrine of Khwaja Moinuddin Chisti in Ajmer, Zardari met with Singh in New Delhi on April 8, 2012, where they both expressed their willingness to find practical and pragmatic solutions to all outstanding issues facing the two countries. Singh stressed that there was need for Pakistan to curb terrorism to enable both countries to make forward movement in a bilateral relationship, and that it was imperative that it brought the perpetrators of the Mumbai attack to justice and prevent terror activities against India from Pakistani soil. Meanwhile, a series of talks were held in the capitals of both countries at different dates between 2011 and 2014. The officials appeared to have made some progress in their deliberations, but no issue was resolved by 2014 as Pakistan failed to undertake a credible trial of the Mumbai attack conspirators, which India had repeatedly sought for.[32] But with the election of Nawaz Sharif as prime minister in May 2013 in Pakistan and Narendra Modi, a Hindu nationalist, as prime minister in May 2014 in India, Indo-Pak relations erupted into tensions with a halt to the composite dialogue, as Kashmiri insurgency was revived again, although initially, relations had begun with bonhomie of friendship and a pledge to proceed with peace process.

Indo-Pak relations under the Modi government: a roller coaster peace process (2014–16)

During the parliamentary election campaign, as leader of the Hindu nationalist party BJP, Narendra Modi took a hardline stance against Pakistan and opposed Article 370, but, after his party's landslide victory, Modi softened his position. To demonstrate his desire of seeking friendly relations with Pakistan and other neighbors, he invited Sharif along with the other heads of the SAARC nations to his swearing-in ceremony as prime minister in May 2014. Modi and Sharif expressed bonhomie for each other, and they agreed to begin bilateral talks announcing that their foreign secretaries were scheduled to meet at the end of August in New Delhi. But that meeting was canceled as India took objection to Pakistan's high commissioner to India Abdul Basit's invitation to Kashmir All Parties Hariyat Conference (APHC) separatist leaders to meet him at his residence in New Delhi for independence celebrations on August 14, a practice to which previous governments had turned a blind eye for many years in the past.[33] The cancelation of talks produced a distinct chill between Modi and Sharif when they failed to hold bilateral talks at the attendance of the SAARC summit held in Kathmandu, Nepal, in November 2014. However, on the eve of the February 2015 cricket World Cup matches, Modi engaged in a cricket diplomacy by calling Sharif and other leaders of the SAARC nations and wished them luck while indicating that his foreign secretary would soon visit their capitals. Modi thus sent a signal that he wanted to revive talks with Pakistan.[34] On the first leg of his whirlwind trip of South Asian states, on March 3, 2015, foreign secretary S. Jaishankar met with his counterpart Aizaz Ahmad Chaudhury for talks in Islamabad and described that they were held in a "constructive and positive atmosphere" with "expressing a determination to forge a cooperative relationship with Pakistan." They talked about bilateral relations and the need for the speedy trials of the Mumbai conspirators and to maintain peace and tranquility along the LOC as vital to sustain the talks, as India accused Pakistan of repeated ceasefire violations.[35] Attending the summit of the Shanghai Cooperation Organization (SCO) in Ufa, Russia, Modi and Sharif met on the sidelines and issued a joint statement agreeing to a meeting of their national security advisors (NSA) in New Delhi in August to discuss all issues connected to "terrorism." Modi agreed to attend the forthcoming November 2015 SAARC meeting scheduled to be held in Islamabad, Pakistan. But as terrorists struck in Gurdaspur, Punjab, on July 17 and Udhampur, Kashmir, on August 5, 2015, it reinforced New Delhi's insistence that the talks should be about terrorism. So, as the August meeting of NSAs approached, in response to domestic criticism that Kashmir was not included in the Modi-Sharif joint statement and that only terrorism was mentioned, Pakistan's NSA Sartaj Aziz invited Hurriyat leaders for a reception at Pakistan's high commissioner's residency in New Delhi, to which the Modi government strongly objected. Because of India's precondition of discussing the issue of terrorism first, Aziz canceled his trip a day before the scheduled meeting.[36] In November 2015, Modi and Sharif met again on the sidelines of the climate change conference held in Paris and announced the resumption of dialogue between the two countries. Subsequently, on December 6, 2015, the Indo-Pakistan NSAs – Ajit Kumar Doval and Nasser Khan Janjua – met in Bangkok, Thailand, and held talks covering peace and security, Kashmir, terrorism and tranquility along the LOC.[37] This meeting was followed by India's External Affairs Minister Sushma Swaraj's visit to Islamabad to attend the "Heart of Asia conference," an aid conference for Afghanistan in early December 2015, where she met Pakistan's Foreign Affairs Advisor Sartaj Aziz and held talks with him. In their joint statement, they "condemned terrorism, and resolved to eliminate it" and said that Pakistan had given assurances on an "early completion of the Mumbai trial." They also announced that they had agreed to resume a structured dialogue called the "Comprehensive Bilateral Dialogue," covering ten issues including terrorism and humanitarian issues.[38] On December 25, on a visit to Kabul to inaugurate the Indian-built Afghan parliament, Modi, en route to New Delhi, made a surprise stopover visit to Lahore, ostensibly to attend Sharif's grand-daughter's wedding and to personally wish Sharif a happy birthday. Modi was warmly received by Sharif and they both embraced each other. Later they held an hour-long discussion at Sharif's Raiwind residence on how to improve people-to-people ties and agreed that the peace process must move forward to resolve their problems so that the two countries can "tackle the challenges of poverty together." The visit was characterized as "imaginative diplomacy" and a "bold and laudable initiative" for improving bilateral relations between India and Pakistan.[39] But predictably, with intent to derail the peace process on January 2, 2016, five terrorists attacked the Pathankot airbase near the border with Pakistan, in which during three days of fighting seven Indian soldiers and five terrorists were killed. The Pakistan-based United Jihad Council, a coalition of Kashmiri militants led by Mohammad Salahuddin who has been declared a "global terrorist" by the US, claimed the attack while India blamed the JEM, led by Masood Azhar. But as the terrorists might have expected, Modi did not react angrily, nor did he call off the talks. Instead, Modi called for restraint on the part of his colleagues and suggested that they wait for the Sharif government's response. This time, the Sharif government went beyond a routine condemning of the terrorist attack in that it offered to follow the leads provided by New Delhi and investigate the incident jointly with India. Sharif talked to Modi on the phone and his NSA General Janjua spoke to his counterpart Doval.

Subsequently, India and Pakistan formed a Joint Investigation Team (JIT), and at the end of March, the Pakistan investigators visited Pathankot. But, to India's surprise, on April 7, Pakistan abruptly suspended the dialogue saying that India was attempting to put the Kashmir issue on the backburner and refused to reciprocate the joint investigation by inviting Indian investigators to Pakistan.[40] With the revival of the Kashmiri uprising in July 2016 followed by the September Uri attack, relations led to deepening tensions between the two countries.

Revival of Kashmiri uprising and the Uri terror attack produce deepening tensions (2014–17)

On July 8, 2016, Burhan Muzaffar Wani, a commander of the Hizbul Mujahideen, a Kashmiri militant group, was killed by the Indian security forces in a gun battle. The next day, thousands of his supporters attended his funeral in his home village of Trail in south Kashmir. Immediately following Wani's death, an uprising broke out with thousands of protesters thronging streets in towns across the Kashmir Valley, leading to clashes between them and the Indian security forces. The violence in the Valley was the worst in years, leaving more than thirty dead and thousands injured by the end of the week. Beginning July 9, the security forces began using pellet guns against the protesters, who started attacking police vehicles, security posts and government property, as well as throwing stones at the security forces. But even with frequent curfews, mass arrests and harsh treatment of protesters by the security forces with its heavy presence in the Valley failed to end the raging rebellion. This heavy-handed approach by the security forces and its brutal use of force against the young protestors only led to further alienation among the youth, and they began demanding self-rule or independence. The protesters often began raising Pakistani flags with pro-Pakistan slogans. And the odd coalition of PDP-BJP (the PDP is sympathetic to protesters and seeks autonomy, while the BJP, a Hindu nationalist party, seeks complete integration of Kashmir with India and revocation of Article 370) government, first led by Chief Minister Mufti Mohammed Sayeed and later by his daughter Mehbooba Mufti after his death in 2015, failed to end the militancy, as this coalition only engendered suspicion among the protestors about the center's intensions.[41] In the wake of this uprising, on August 14, 2016, commemorating the 70th independence day and addressing the nation, Pakistan's president at that time, Mamnoon Hussain, touched on the Kashmir issue and said, "Pakistan cannot forget Kashmiris and would continue to support them to get right of self-determination in light of the UN resolutions."[42] The following day, on August 15, celebrating India's independence day, in his address to the nation, Modi retorted by saying that ever since he had asked the Pakistani establishment to look at human rights abuses in Baluchistan, Gilgit-Baltistan (Pakistan designated it as the fifth province of Pakistan in March 2017, separating it from POK), he had been flooded with messages of gratitude from the people of these areas, and "I am grateful to these people who have thanked me in the past few days. If people of Baluchistan thank me, they are thanking the 125 crore (1.25 billion) Indians."[43] This statement by Modi angered Pakistan greatly. Baluchistan is a province of Pakistan in which the leader of the Baloch Republican Party (BRP), Brahamdagh Bugti, had been fighting for independence, but then he applied for asylum in India.

In the midst of the continuing Kashmiri insurgency, on September 18, 2016, four heavily armed terrorists, in a suicide attack on an army camp close to the headquarters of the 12th Brigade at Uri in Baramulla district, Kashmir, killed seventeen soldiers and wounded nineteen. This was one of the deadliest attacks on the security forces in recent times by terrorists who were believed to have infiltrated across the LOC from POK.[44] Immediately thereafter, by condemning this terror attack as "cowardly," Modi assured the nation that those who were behind the "despicable" strike would not go unpunished.[45] In wake of these terror attacks, in a survey conducted by the Pew Research center, 62% of Indians favored using an overwhelming military force as the best way to defeat terrorism.[46] Attending his party's National Council meeting in Kozhikode, Kerala state, on September 24, Modi launched a blistering attack on Pakistan. He said,

> in the last few months, our neighbor tried to destroy our country by exporting terrorists more than 17 times. But our army defeated them. More than 110 terrorists have been killed in the past few months by the Indian army while they were trying to infiltrate.

He contemptuously declared, "India exports software, Pakistan exports terror."[47] In response, on September 24, on his stopover in London en route to New York to attend the UN, Sharif told the reporters, "the Uri can be reaction of atrocities in Kashmir, as the close relatives and near and dear ones of those killed and blinded over the last two months," and criticized India for blaming Pakistan without evidence.[48] On September 25 in his monthly radio program talk, Modi reiterated that the terror strike will be punished, and at the same time, he told the people of Kashmir that "peace, unity, and harmony" are the ways to resolve problems, and expressed confidence that all issues can be addressed through discussions.[49]

As it has been already warned, on September 28 and 29, the special forces of the Indian army launched "surgical strikes" in a five-hour-long operation and destroyed seven terror pads across the LOC in POK, killing scores of terrorists. India's director-general of military operations (DGMO) Lt. Gen. Ranbir Singh confirmed the strikes to the Indian media, and perhaps to stress India's limited intensions, he also informed his Pakistani counterpart, although Pakistan denied that there was any such military strike by India, and said that there have been border firing initiated and conducted by India which is an "existential phenomenon." Singh later issued a full statement to explain why the strikes were undertaken.[50] Even before the surgical strike was undertaken, in an interview telecast on September 26, Pakistan Defense Minister Khawaja Muhammad Asif threatened to unleash nukes against India, saying, "if our safety is threatened we will annihilate them (India), and we have not produced tactical weapons to be just be as showpieces."[51] This threat by Asif received a public smackdown by Obama administration officials for loose talk about using nuclear weapons against India. US State Department spokesman Mark Toner said, "nuclear capable states have a very clear responsibility to exercise restraint regarding nuclear weapons and missile capabilities," and the assault on the army headquarters in Uri, he said, was part of the cross-border terrorism emanating from Pakistan.[52] National Security Advisor Susan Rice called her Indian counterpart Ajit Doval and endorsed India's stand on cross-border terrorism. And her office released a statement critical of Pakistan, saying the US expects Islamabad to "take effective action" to combat terrorist groups.[53] On October 16, in his public comment after the surgical strike, Modi noted, "compulsion of time and requirements of a situation can render war unavoidable," although India has always preferred Buddha (peace).[54] At a summit of the heads of state of the BRICS countries (Brazil, Russia, India, China and South Africa) who met in Goa, India, on October 16, while reminding the leaders that the growing arc of terrorism was threatening the Middle East, West Asia, Europe and South Asia, without mentioning its name, Modi attacked Pakistan by calling it "the mother-ship of terrorism." Modi added, "in our region, terrorism poses a grave threat to peace, security, and development. Tragically, the mother-ship of terrorism is a country in India's neighborhood (and) its terror modules around the world are linked to this mother-ship."[55] Responding to India's attempt to isolate Pakistan, speaking at the Indian Institute of Peace and Conflict Studies in New Delhi, on October 24, the then Pakistani high commissioner to India, Abdul Basit, slammed India by questioning, "how on earth is it possible to isolate a country on terrorism when that country itself is the worst victim of terrorism." Basit said Kashmir was the "root cause of all problems between the two countries and that Pakistan does not need (India's) misplaced jingoism, and hyper nationalism" to pursue its foreign policy objectives.[56] On a visit to Manama, the capital of Bahrain, on October 25, India's Home Minister Rajnath Singh met with King Hamad bin Salman Al Khalifa and shared India's concern over terrorism and repeated the accusation that Pakistan uses terrorism as an instrument of state policy towards India.[57] Following the Uri terror attack, to Pakistan's frustration and slight, India announced that it would not attend the November 2016, 19th SAARC summit scheduled to be held in Islamabad, and to its dismay, other members such as Bangladesh, Sri Lanka, Bhutan and Afghanistan also followed suit.[58] To further heighten tensions, in the aftermath of the Uri terror attack, Modi called for the review of the 1960 Indus Water Treaty signed by Nehru and Ayub Khan by stating that "blood and water cannot go together" over Pakistan's repeated cross-border terrorist attacks, (and) the latest being the Uri attack. The Modi government claimed that India was using only its 20% share of waters allocated to it by the treaty. It said that it wanted to restart the Tulbul navigation project on the Jhelum River, which was previously suspended in the wake of Pakistan's objection. India wanted to make use of its rights in the western rivers for agriculture, storage and hydroelectric power for the states of Punjab and J&K, a claim which Pakistan challenged and objected to, as it would cause irreparable damage to its farming, drinking and hydroelectric projects. The Indian and Pakistani water commissions, which meet twice a year, were mandated to resolve their dispute, but this time, India refused to participate due to Pakistan-supported cross-border terror attacks. Pakistan appealed to the World Bank and the US to intervene to settle the dispute.[59]

The sentencing of Kulbhushan Jadhav to death for his alleged spy activities in Baluchistan province by Pakistani secret military court, approved by the Pakistan's army chief Qamar Javed Bajwa, was apparently unknown to Prime Minister Sharif in April 2017. This episode further added to the escalation of tensions between the two countries. The Indian Ministry of External Affairs reacted sharply to Jadhav's death sentence, protesting to Pakistan's high commissioner that "the government and people of India will regard it as a case of premeditated murder" if it is carried out and that the conviction was farcical, as it was done on trumped-up charges secretly by a military court without even allowing Jadhav access to India's consular services. India claims that Jadhav, a retired naval officer, was abducted from the Iran-Afghanistan border in March 2016 by the ISI and was subsequently subjected to farcical trial and conviction. This claim by India was authenticated by former German ambassador to Pakistan Gunter Mulack, who, speaking at a seminar in Karachi on May 16, 2017, said that Jadhav was picked up by the Taliban from near the Baluchistan-Afghanistan border and sold to the ISI, and that the Pakistan army decided to arrest and try Jadhav to undermine Sharif's attempt to probe the involvement of Pakistani nationals in the Pathankot terror attack, as well as to counter India's campaign against cross-border terrorism. But the Pakistan army asserts that Jadhav had confessed and that he was assigned by India's spy agency – the RAW (Research and Analysis Wing) – to undertake espionage and sabotage activities in restive Baluchistan and in the city of Karachi. The Pakistani military released video of his confession.[60] India took Jadhav's issue to the International Court of Justice at Hague in early May and obtained a stay order until the case is debated and resolved by it. Pakistan agreed to the order, although it said it is not bound by the world court's order.[61] As of this writing, the court has agreed to hear the case.

Meanwhile, the UN Committee Against Torture published a report expressing concern over the Pakistan government "authorizing its military courts to try civilians on terrorism-related offences," and the panel has asked Islamabad to "end the resort to military courts for terrorism, and provide the opportunity for appeals in civilian courts of cases involving civilians already adjudicated under military jurisdiction." Thus, the report delegitimized the verdict against Jadhav.[62] On May 27, a petition was filed before the Pakistan Supreme Court by an advocate named Farooq Naek, a leader of opposition party, the PPP, asking the apex court to order the immediate execution of Jadhav under domestic laws.[63] If the execution is carried out by Pakistan by ignoring the legal opinion of the World Court, Indo-Pak relations are likely to turn much worse than they have had ever been.

The Kashmiri Muslim insurgency continues unabated

As noted earlier, stone throwing continues unabated by young men and women with the raising of Azadi (freedom) and pro-Pakistan slogans accompanied by frequent calls for strikes and shutdowns. To deal with this insurgency, as already noted, the Indian security forces have used pellet guns, which resulted in the killing and blinding of hundreds of protesters. The security forces even began to use the Kashmiris as human shields to discourage stone throwing by the protesters. In the face of heavy criticism by human rights organizations for using pellet guns against protesters, the security forces have declared that they would explore the use of other options, such as the use of PAVA shells and rubber bullets. Unlike in the past, a wider section of the Indian media and the elites have turned against the Kashmiri militants, supporting the heavy-handed treatment of the protesters by looking askance at India's democratic norms and practices under the Modi's Hindu nationalist government.[64] Ironically, this time, the movement in the Valley, for the most part, has turned mostly Islamist. For example, unlike most of the Hurriyat leaders who seek either independence or autonomy, Wani's Hizbul Mujahideen (HM) advocates joining

Pakistan, and this position has become popular among a wider segment of the younger population in the Valley. No wonder Zakir Musa, who succeeded Wani and who later left the HM to join Al Qaeda, in an audio slide show threatened to kill the Hurriyat leaders for calling their struggle as political, instead of Islamic, and supported establishing a caliphate in J&K. The Hurriyat leaders have denounced him for giving such a call.[65] Sabzar Bhat, who succeeded Musa, was killed by security forces on May 27, 2017. The security forces imposed a curfew in seven police station areas in the city of Srinagar for time, as a pre-emptive measure to prevent the spread of violence, which already broke out following his killing.[66] The vulnerable sections of Kashmiri society, especially the youth, are being indoctrinated by nearly fifty Saudi and Pakistani channels, preaching through unlicensed TVs to promote their Saudi Wahhabi fundamentalism and Pakistani conservative Islamic theology by stoking the fires of "azadi" rage and anti-India propaganda.[67] As Adil Rasheed notes, the Salafi-jihadi groups, particularly ISIS (Islamic State Iraq and Syria) operatives, are using social media apps like Telegram to denounce the so-called Kashmir independence movement as un-Islamic. Instead, they say, it should be a Jihad to please Allah so as to impose the most Salafized version of Shariah.[68] It is no wonder that a large section of Kashmiris appear to be abandoning the Sufi (pacifist) Hani liberal Islamic theology, which Modi admires, and embracing the Wahhabi brand of Islam. The *Kashmiriyat*, a concept that stresses a distinct Kashmiri identity and a solidarity of different faiths and ethnic groups in the state, has eroded, as illustrated by the expulsion of Hindu Pandits by the militants in the first uprising of the early 1990s and their unwelcome by the militants as the Modi government seeks to resettle them in the Valley. The insurgency has taken on a religious orientation, rather than a nationalistic one. the fact that either Pandits in the Valley, or Hindus in Jammu or Buddhists in Ladakh are not part of the separatist armed struggle. Insurgency is entirely confined to the Valley, which is predominantly Muslim. As R. Jagannathan notes,

> we are essentially witnessing the ISIS-isation of the Kashmir Valley with self-radicalized youths, additionally instigated by Pakistani Deep state, using the "azadi" as a slogan for Islamist mobilization and jihadi violence.

He questions, "where is the scope for insaniyat (humanity) when insanity rules."[69] Responding to Jagannathan's and other Indian elite, Wajahat Qazi, a Kashmiri, notes, "when they spew venom in the garb of liberal opinion, and openly root for repression and oppression of Kashmiris and brand the unrest as one motivated and engineered by Islamist outpouring, it manifests either obfuscation or ignorance." Qazi argues, the current spasm of violence is not merely about what Burhan represented and symbolized for most people; defiance against oppression. If this sought to be curbed, contained, or smothered by ruthless application of force and Machiavellian politics, the future is not difficult to see.

He calls on India for soul searching and for policy review towards Kashmir and to institute a sober conflict resolution approach that redounds to the benefit of all stakeholders – especially the Kashmiris, including Pakistan.[70] Dr. Radha Kumar similarly echoes the sentiment by calling on the Modi government to launch a peace process with Hurriyat leaders right away, instead of following both the center and Chief Minister Mufti, who vowed to not engage them until the insurgency was ended. She points out that a majority of Kashmiris want to live in freedom, peace and dignity just as the majority of Indians do, the stone-throwing pro-Pakistani militants do not represent the Kashmiris, and that Hurriyat leaders, among whom Abdul Ghani, Majid Dar, and Haq Qureshi have been killed by militants in search of peace, should be invited to the peace process.[71] On May 28, in an interaction with the media, India's army chief General Bipin Rawat said that India was fighting a "proxy war" in Kashmir, which is a "dirty war," and therefore Indian security forces have had to fight through "innovative" ways, and he defended the use of human shields by security forces.[72] On May 7, Chief Minister Mufti expressed an optimistic note by saying that Modi can resolve the Kashmiri issue. Speaking at the inauguration of a fly-over in Jammu, Mufti said, "if anyone can find a solution to the Jammu & Kashmir problem, it is PM Narendra Modi. He has a strong mandate; whatever decision he makes, the country will support him."[73] As the internal unrest continued in the Valley unabated, on June 3, Home Minister Singh told the media that surgical attacks last year had lasting positive benefits in that there was a 45% reduction of cross-border infiltration.[74] Meanwhile, Hurriyat leaders were accused of being on the payroll of the ISI. On May 2, *The Times of India* contended that it was in possession of intelligence documents showing that Hurriyat leaders were on the payroll of ISI and others who were involved in anti-India activities.[75] Nearly ten months after the protests had broken out following Wani's killing, the National Investigation Agency (NIA) launched a probe of hardline separatist leaders, including Syed Ali Shah Geelani, Naeem Khan, Farooq Ahmed Dar, Gazi Javed Baba and others, for allegedly receiving funds from Pakistan-based Hafiz Saeed's LET and the ISI.[76] In early June 2017, the agency raided residences and offices of Hurriyat leaders. In response, in a joint statement the leaders criticized the Modi government and alleged that the NIA has been given the task "just to drag and involve Hurriyat leadership into fabricated cases to pressurize the leadership" and that "all these state-sponsored tactics won't deter us from pursuing our mission, nor these coercions, suppressive and aggressive measures will make us surrender."[77] Subsequently, in late July, the NIA arrested and charged Naeem Khan, Bitta Karate, the commander of JKLF, Altaf Ahmad Shah, the son-in-law of Geelani, and four others over Pakistan funding of terror. The NIA did not rule out further arrests.[78] The charging of the Hurriyat leaders that they are receiving funds from Pakistan may discredit them as credible interlocutors on behalf of the Kashmiris. Meanwhile, recognizing that military approach alone would not end the Kashmir imbroglio, in late October, the Modi government announced a policy shift to open talks with the separatist leaders by appointing Dineshwar Sharma, the former Intelligence Bureau director, to open dialogue with all the stakeholders beginning in December. Modi said the region's problems could be solved by "embracing its people rather than resorting to abuse or bullets," and Sharma said that he will "talk to all people in an effort to bring about a solution" to Kashmir.[79] But the Hurriyat leadership rejected the dialogue by saying that the center's move was an eyewash. It issued a statement saying that Sharma was coming to "restore peace rather than addressing the dispute, and limits the scope of any engagement with him and make it an exercise in futility."[80] In the midst of ongoing insurgency and India's security forces' crackdown to squelch it, the then Prime Minister Sharif launched a futile campaign to gain international support against India.

Shari's campaign against India on behalf of Kashmir militants fails

On September 22, 2016, addressing the UN General Assembly in New York, Sharif said a new generation of Kashmiris has started a freedom struggle against India.

> Burhan Wani, the young leader murdered by Indian forces, has emerged as the symbol of the latest Kashmiri intifada, a popular and peaceful freedom movement led by Kashmiris, young and old, men and women, armed only with an undying faith and legitimacy of their cause and hunger for freedom in their hearts [and] this indigenous uprising of the Kashmiris has been met, as usual, with brutal repression by India's occupation force of over half a million soldiers.

Sharif called on the UN to undertake consultations with India, Pakistan and the true representatives of the Kashmiri people to implement the resolutions of the Security Council.[81] He held talks with almost every world leader on the sidelines of the UN session and raised the issue with the leaders of the US, UK, Japan and Turkey. For example, Sharif and the Turkish President

Tayyip Erdogan agreed to the Organization of Islamic Cooperation (OIC) sending a fact-finding mission to Kashmir. However, he failed to gain support for his cause among world leaders. For example, the outgoing UN Secretary General Ban Ki Moon said UN "good offices" are available only if both India and Pakistan have requested it. The then US Secretary of State John Kerry told Sharif that Pakistan must stop giving safe haven to terrorists and cap its nuclear arsenal, instead of agreeing to mediate the conflict. Even the all-weather friend China distanced itself from Sharif's call for support on Kashmir other than calling for peaceful settlement through dialogue.[82] As Vivek Chadha et al. point out, although Sharif had sought to internationalize the Kashmir issue, he failed in his mission, as India quickly rallied international support from the US, UK, Germany, Japan, South Korea and the members of the OIC for its surgical strikes following the Uri terrorist attack that implicated Pakistan, instead of supporting his plea on behalf of the Kashmiris at the world body.[83] Ahead of his diplomatic endeavor at the UN, in August, Sharif had also dispatched twenty-two parliamentarians as special envoys to plead the cause of Kashmiris in world capitals.[84] In her rebuttal to Sharif's tirade against India, India's External Affairs' Swaraj accused Pakistan of naked support for terrorism and called on the world community to join India into adopting a global strategy to defeat it. She said, "there is a living proof of Pakistan's complicity in cross-border terror" as confessed by Bahadur Ali, a terrorist of the Uri attack who is in India's custody.

> But when confronted with such evidence, Pakistan remains in self-denial. It persists in the belief that such attacks will enable it obtain the territory it covets. And my firm advice to Pakistan is; abandon this dream. Let me state unequivocally that Jammu and Kashmir is an integral part of India and will always remain so.

Responding to Sharif's allegations of India's human rights abuses, Swaraj said they are baseless, and "those accusing of human rights violations would do well to introspect and see what egregious abuses they are perpetrating in their own country, including Baluchistan. The brutality against the Baloch people represents the worst form of state repression." As Sharif has accused India of brutality, Swaraj said, it did not put any preconditions for peace talks.[85] As Umair Jamali notes, Pakistan's decades-long policy of naked meddling in Indian J&K has undermined Indo-Pak relations. He quotes Michael Kugelman of the Woodrow Wilson International Center for Scholars, who said, "In fact, Pakistan's official rhetoric of extending moral, diplomatic support has been fueled by its support for Islamist militant groups in the region, which has only delegitimized the Kashmiri struggle." There is no military

solution to the conflict, and both sides recognize that any mutually acceptable solution has to come through diplomacy. Jamali quotes Aqil Shah, who
said, "the most feasible option is to accept the LOC as an international border, demilitarize on both sides, and allow the free movement of people and
commerce across the border."[86] The former Pakistan ambassador to the US,
Touqir Hussain, points out that India-Pakistan relations are doomed given
the stubborn reality of the current relationship between the Modi and Sharif
governments. He notes, following the terrorist attacks in Pathankot and Uri
by the Jihadists, the nationalist Modi government has spurned dialogue with
Pakistan and has launched an intense campaign to isolate it in the region
and beyond by injecting fresh irritants in the relations, such as the issues of
Baluchistan and the Indus Waters Treaty. In response, as Hussain observes,
Pakistan has hit back against India. "Imbued with overwhelming confidence
in the China Pakistan Economic Corridor (CPEC), in its geostrategic value,
and reliance on its military strength to which has been added tactical nuclear
weapons capability, Pakistan has not been unnerved." Furthermore, he notes,
because of India's hostility, the Jihadists enjoy a great deal of support among
the right-wing elements of Pakistani society, and as a result, the government
is reluctant to act against them. In addition, Hussain points out, Pakistan has
joined an alliance with Russia, China and the Taliban against India's interests in Afghanistan.[87] Although, after a casual meeting with Sharif on the
margins of the SCO summit held in Astana, Kazakhstan, June 11–12, 2017,
the Modi government announced the release of eleven civil prisoners from
Indian jails as a "good will gesture,"[88] India's gesture did not result in a thaw
in relations with Pakistan, given their intense mutual hostility over Kashmir.
Meanwhile, in late July 2017 the Pakistan Supreme Court disqualified Sharif
over corruption charges, forcing him to resign. And Shahid Khaqan Abbasi,
Minister for Petroleum and Natural Resources in Sharif's cabinet, became
an interim prime minister until the July 2018 parliamentary elections were to
be held. But as militant attacks increased in J&K, and as ceasefire violations
increased by both sides, accompanied by the displacement of people living
on the border area and including civilian and military casualties, the Modi
government softened its posture, and on the eve of Ramadan, on May 29,
2018, it declared that it would maintain the 2003 ceasefire agreement on the
LOC and international border with Pakistan.[89] Despite this declaration, it did
not end the ceasefire violations and they continued on. For example, as of July
30, 2018, India's cease-fire violations stood at 1,432, while Pakistan's stood at
1,400 by August 9, 2018.[90] The relations continued to remain frozen under a
new Prime Minister Abbasi too. Meanwhile in June 2018, the J&K coalition
government headed by Mufti broke down as its coalition partner BJP withdrew
from the odd coalition, abruptly prompting her to resign. Chief Minister Ram
Madhav, General Secretary of the BJP, offered his reasons for withdrawing

from the three-year coalition when he faced reporters in New Delhi. He said, "terrorism, violence and radicalism have risen, and the fundamental rights of the citizens are under danger in the Kashmir Valley" and that the coalition had not helped to curb a deteriorating security situation in the state. Addressing a news conference, Mufti said, "We tried our best for dialogue and reconciliation" but "unfortunately, we did not get an appropriate response from the other side."[91] As a consequence, on the orders of India's President Ram Nath Kovind, the legislature was suspended, and the governor's rule headed by N. N. Vohra was established. In August 2018 Vohra, an expert on Kashmir and a non-political bureaucrat, was replaced by its party man Satya Pal Malik as the state governor, which is likely to alienate the Kashmiris further because he is a BJP member. In the same month, militants assassinated Shujaat Bukhari, the editor of *Rising Kashmir* and a moderate who had called for reconciliation with India.

On June 14, 2018, the UN Human Rights Commissioner Zeid Raad Al Hussein issued a very critical report of India's human rights abuses in Kashmir, including Pakistan's in POK, and called for international inquiry to investigate the abuses being committed by Indian security forces. He cites numerous examples of security forces using excessive force in committing unlawful killings and a high number of injuries, sexual violence and kidnappings with impunity. He urged the Indian government to repeal the AFSPA of 1990 and J&K Public Safety Act of 1978. By calling the terrorists "armed Groups," the report cites evidence of them committing a wide range of human rights abuses too, including kidnappings, killings of civilians and sexual violence since late 1980s.[92] This was the first report ever produced by the UN human rights commission on Kashmir, which again tarnished India's image as a democratic state in world opinion. But instead of acknowledging and pledging to address some of the abuses raised by the report, the Indian Ministry of External Affairs (MEA) swiftly reacted angrily by stating that it was a "selective compilation of largely unverified information," and "It was fallacious (and) overtly prejudicial" seeking "to build a false narrative by violating India's" sovereignty and integrity.[93]

Meanwhile, in July 2018 in Pakistan, Imran Khan, a famous cricketer turned politician, and the founder of the Pakistan Tehreek-e-Insaf (PTI – Movement for Justice) Party became prime minister by winning in parliamentary elections.

Khan calls for dialogue with India, but fails to break the ice so far (July 2018–present)

Even before he assumed the office of prime minister, in his first speech after declaring his victory, Imran Khan said, "We want to improve relations with India if its leadership also wants it. This blame game that whatever goes wrong in Pakistan is because of India and vice-versa brings us back to square one," and "if they take one step towards us, we will take two, but at least we need a start."[94] Following his victory, Modi spoke to him congratulating him, and expressed hope that democracy would take deeper roots in Pakistan. Modi reiterated his vision of peace and development in the entire neighborhood.[95] Coincidently with Khan's election, Modi softened his stance on Kashmir. For example, on August 15, in his India's Independence Day speech to the nation, Modi said,

> Whether it is of Ladakh or Jammu or Kashmir Valley, there should be balanced development. All expectations of the people there should be fulfilled, infrastructure should be strengthened and we should walk with everyone. We don't want to move in the path of guns and abuse.

Modi added, "Atal ji (the former late Prime Minister Vajpayee) called for insaniyat (humanity), kashmiriat (Kashmiri culture) and jamhooriyat (democracy). I also said the issues in Kashmir can be resolved by embracing the people of Kashmir."[96] However, Modi is yet to translate this pledge into a policy performance on Kashmir to end the conflict.

Upon assumption of office as prime minister, in September Khan wrote a letter to Modi calling for the renewal of peace dialogue between the two countries. Khan specifically sought a meeting between his Foreign Minister Shah Mahmood Qureshi and his counterpart Swaraj on the sidelines of the UN General Assembly meeting when they arrived in New York.[97] The Modi government immediately responded by agreeing to have its Foreign Minister Swaraj meet her counterpart Qureshi in New York. However, its foreign ministry spokesperson Raveesh Kumar stressed that the session would be a "meeting not a dialogue" and did not represent the assumption of regular high-level government talks.[98] But a day later India called off the planned meeting. Kumar gave a reason, saying that the meeting was called off because of the killing of Indian security personnel by Pakistan-based enemies and for Pakistan's releasing of postage stamps in honor of Burhan Wani, glorifying his terrorism in Kashmir. Indian opposition parties also criticized the decision to hold talks after rebels in the Valley killed the border guard and later raided over a dozen homes of police officers, abducting three and killing them. The Pakistan Foreign Minister Qureshi regretted India's decision, saying that Pakistan wanted peace and stability in the region, but India was perhaps more motivated by its internal politics. Pakistan Information Minister Fawad Chaudhry said, "an extremist segment in India doesn't want to see Pakistan and India move ahead on the path of dialogue to resolve issues."[99] Upset by this abrupt cancelation, Khan decried the decision and obliquely criticized Modi, saying that he was

> disappointed at the arrogant and negative response by India to may call for resumption of the peace dialogue. [H]owever, all my life I have come across small men occupying big offices who do not have the vision to see the larger picture.[100]

On September 22, addressing the media, India's army chief General Rawat called for a fitting reply for murdering Indian security personnel by Pakistan. He said,

> We need to take stern action to avenge the barbarism that terrorists and the Pakistan Army have been carrying out. Yes, it is time to give it back to them in the same coin, [and] not resorting to similar kind of barbarism. But I think the other side must also feel the same pain.[101]

Responding to Rawat's threat, on September 23, the Pakistan Army spokesperson Major General Asif Ghafoor said, "We are ready for war but choose to walk the path of peace in the interest of the people of Pakistan, the neighbors and the region." He noted, "the Indian army has failed to clamp down the political struggle of Kashmiris" and Pakistan's offer for talks still on the table. General Ghafoor warned that New Delhi should stop war mongering and "not take the nuclear armed state's overtures for peace as weakness" and "should stop trying its patience."[102] In late September at the UN session, both foreign ministers traded insults when they addressed the assembly. Swaraj accused Pakistan of harboring terrorists. She said, "terrorism is bred not in some faraway land, but across our border to the west, [and] neighbor's expertise is not restricted to spawning grounds for terrorism, [but] it is also an expert in trying to mask malevolence with verbal duplicity." But she did not rule out peace talks, saying, "In response, Qureshi accused India that it called off dialogue the third time by 'the Modi government, each time on flimsy grounds' (and) they prefer politics over peace. No longer can the excuse of terrorism be used to systematically oppress the Pakistani people."[103] Very soon, Modi renewed his hawkish stance with Khan as prime minister. For instance, on October 1, in his monthly radio program "Mann ki Baat," Modi warned Pakistan of a befitting reply for ceasefire violations. He said,

> It has been decided to that our soldiers will give a befitting reply to whoever makes an attempt to destroy the atmosphere of peace and progress in our nation. We believe in peace, we are committed to taking

it forward, but not at the cost of compromising our self-respect and sovereignty of our nation.[104]

As of this writing, relations continue to be tense, even with Khan's overtures for better relations. It remains to be seen if this Indo-Pak stalemate can ever be broken. We want to proffer some explanations the persistence of this conflict between India and Pakistan over the state of Kashmir and suggest a possible solution for consideration by the parties to end this costly and festering conflict.

Explanations for the persistence of the Kashmir conflict

Both nations claim the same territory

India

India makes a legal claim to the state of J&K on various grounds. It argues that Indian troops entered the state of J&K only after King Singh had signed the Instrument of Accession to fight Pakistan's invasion of the state in October 1947. This was a standard procedure, under which the princely states were given the option of joining either India or Pakistan, which Ali Jinnah violated by sending troops into the state. Besides, the popular and secular leader Sheikh Abdullah of the NC Party supported the accession, believing that the state was better off under a secular and democratic India with the state enjoying a Special Status under Article 370 of the Indian constitution. Although Abdullah subsequently, beginning in 1953, changed his stance and demanded self-determination, in 1975 he accepted the state's integration with India. Although Nehru accepted the principle of plebiscite under UNSC resolutions, India contends his cooperation was contingent on Pakistan's withdrawal from the entire POK, which the latter refused to do. Therefore, Nehru treated the February 1954 state constituent assembly's resolution declaring the state's accession to final as equivalent to a plebiscite. Furthermore, Nehru could not envision ceding his ancestral land to Pakistan, and he sought to demonstrate India's commitment to secularism and democracy by keeping a predominantly Muslim state as an integral part of India. Not only that, Nehru and his successor leaders could not afford to back away from protecting the nearly 3% percent of Hindu Pandits of the Kashmir Valley and predominantly Hindu and Buddhist populations in Jammu and Ladakh regions respectively who wanted to be part of India. But in Pakistan, the less than 3% of Hindus and Christians are under constant assault and persecution, and many Hindus are fleeing to India seeking asylum. A majority of Muslims in the Kashmir Valley, despite their sense of alienation from India, do not want to be part of Pakistan. For example, in a poll conducted by UK-based Market and Opinion International (MORI) in June 2002, 61% of Kashmiris said they are better off remaining as part of India, while only 6% choose to be part of Pakistan if they cannot have the choice of being independent, a choice not sanctioned by 1948 UNSC resolutions.[105] As has been mentioned earlier, the Hindus in Jammu and Buddhists in Ladakh do not want to be part of Pakistan. In addition, India considers the state strategically vital to its security vis-à-vis Pakistan and China. Also, the Indus River system, which consists of six rivers that originate in North India and flow through J&K, constitutes a lifeline for both India and Pakistan, and India cannot afford to part with it.

Under the April 1949 Karachi Indo-Pak agreement, Pakistan-occupied Kashmir (POK) was divided into two entities – Azad Kashmir and the Northern Areas (now called Gilgit-Baltistan). While Azad is granted a self-rule under its 1974 interim constitution, the Northern Areas are brought under Pakistan's direct rule in violation of UNSC resolutions. India contends that Pakistan controls Azad Kashmir (POK) with no real democratic freedoms and commits many human rights abuses, which Pakistan accuses of India in Kashmir, and uses the POK as a training ground for terrorists to fight across the border in India, which the people in POK resent. For example, in early October 2016, residents of the POK protested against Islamabad by stating that their lives had been made a living hell by the keeping of terrorist camps in their midst.[106] On October 1, 2016, the residents of Kotli of the POK took to the streets protesting against the atrocities committed by the Pakistan army and the ISI against the pro-Azadi leaders who do not agree with Pakistan. They demanded an independent investigation into the arrest of Arif Shahid, the chair of the All Parties National Alliance (APNA) and the president of the J&K National Liberation Conference (J&KNLC), who was later murdered in Rawalpindi on May 14, 2013.[107] On October 22, 2016, observing a "black day," the day Pakistan sent its army into Kashmir, the United Kashmir Peoples National Party (UKPNP) urged Pakistan to hold peace talks with India and withdraw from Gilgit-Baltistan and the POK.[108] Furthermore, in violation of the Karachi agreement and the UNSC resolutions, as noted earlier, in 1963, Pakistan signed the Border Agreement with China, ceding it about 2,050 square miles. And in the face of protests from the citizens of Gilgit-Baltistan, Azad Kashmir, Indian-administered Kashmir and India, Pakistan had ignored these protests and annexed Gilgit-Baltistan and made it as one of the provinces of Pakistan in early 2017, despite the fact it is a disputed territory. Pakistan is also is also settling the Gilgit-Baltistan region with Pakistani citizens. In addition, under a $60 billion Chinese investment, China and Pakistan signed the China-Pakistan Economic Corridor (CPEC) agreement in 2015. As part of the Chinese-initiated One Belt One Road (OBOR) Initiative, the Chinese have launched many infrastructure projects in the Gilgit-Baltistan region, which India vehemently opposes (India refuses to join the OBOR).[109] The Kashmiris in POK feel oppressed by Pakistan and do not want to be part of Pakistan, an issue which India occasionally mentions, unlike Pakistan which harps on the Indian-administered J&K perpetually. It is no wonder that in a poll conducted by the London-based Chatham House in 2010, 44% percent of people in POK favored independence compared with 43% in Indian Kashmir.[110] Although the entire J&K is a disputed state under UNSC resolutions, and therefore requires a plebiscite, ironically, Pakistan calls for self-determination primarily in Indian Kashmir but not in POK.

Although Pakistan has been created on the two-nation theory based on the principle of religion, presumably to ensure the security and democratic rights of Muslims, it appears the theory has been breached. For example, a small number of Muslims (about 6 million), known as Muhajirs (immigrants from India), migrated to Pakistan and had played a vital role in building up of the new country. Today they number about 25 million and feel marginalized and, as such in 1984, under the leadership of Altaf Hussain (currently living in exile in London to escape trial) formed the Muttahida Qaumi Movement (MQM), which seeks autonomy or independence consisting of Karachi and Hyderabad. In addition, the former East Pakistan, now Bangladesh, as discussed earlier seceded from Pakistan in 1971 because of the Punjabi-dominated Pakistani military's brutal crackdown and its unwillingness to hand over power to a democratically elected leader, Mujibur Rahaman.

Pakistan has failed to resolve the ongoing Baluch Separatist rebellion in Baluchistan. The Baluchis account for about 7 million, and the province, which possesses many natural resources, was annexed by Pakistan in 1948. The Baluchis rebelled and fought the Pakistani military five times since 1948. They feel their natural resources are being exploited by the Pakistan federal government, which does not share any of the benefits with them. As a result, nearly 58% of people live below the poverty level and there exists only a 30% literacy rate. The Baluchis formed the Baloch Liberation Army (BLA) and the Baluchistan Liberation United Front (BLUF) with the goal of seeking self-determination. Their popular leader, Nawab Akbar Bugti, was killed by the Pakistan military in 2006. The Baluchi accuse the Pakistan military of committing many egregious human rights abuses such as torture, murder, extrajudicial killing and internal displacement. The Pakistani government has failed to integrate the Baluchis by respecting their dignity and democratic freedoms.[111]

In addition, Pakistan has become an epicenter of terrorism. Thousands of Jihadists are being produced by the Saudi-funded madrasaas which number in the hundreds and are making the country ungovernable and unstable, as the government has failed to reign them in. Pakistan was at one time a moderate country, but after General Zia seized power in a military coup in 1977, he sought to transform the country into an Islamist state by introducing Sharia courts, blasphemy and Hudud Laws (Quran-based punishments), as well as by promoting the establishment of hundreds of madrassas where Jihadists are being produced. Terrorists have killed nearly 60,000 people in the last 20 years.[112] There are twelve domestic, thirty-two transnational and four extremist groups in Pakistan.[113] In October 2017, Pakistan authorities froze 5,100 accounts of terrorist suspects, including the accounts of the LET and JEM under the Ant-Terrorism Act (ATA). Both these groups have caused havoc in the country.[114]

Ali Jinnah, the founder of Pakistan, was a secular leader who nominally belonged to the Shia sect. But ironically, his sect, who account for about 14%–20% of the Pakistani population, have become the victims of a Sunni assault led by sects such as Lashkar-e-Jhangvi (LEJ) and Sipah-e-Sahaba-e-Pakistan (SSP, now known as Ahle Sunnat Wal Jamaat – ASWJ). For example, in 2013 alone, as Dr. Christine Fair notes, 700 Shia were killed and more than 1,000 were injured in more than 200 sectarian terrorist attacks. And since 2000 through 2014, nearly 4,000 Shia have been killed and 6,800 injured, showing a serious sectarian divide in the country.[115] And the five million Ahmadis who revere their founder, Mirza Ghulam Ahmed, as a kind of prophet, have been declared as non-Muslims under the 1973 Pakistan constitution and are oppressed by both the government and other Muslims. Given these interminable problems facing the country, in 2010, *Foreign Policy* ranked Pakistan as a failing state ranking below several African countries, Afghanistan and Iraq.[116] Therefore, to assume that people in J&K will opt to join Pakistan is an unrealistic and farfetched idea. For these reasons, India claims J&K as its state.

Pakistan

Pakistan claims that the two-nation theory still holds good the fact that it remains a sovereign country of 200 million people with the fifth largest military force in the world and possessing nuclear weapons. Under this two-nation principle, therefore, Pakistan has a legitimate claim to J&K as it is predominantly Muslim, and as India had agreed to conduct plebiscite under UNSC resolutions to decide for themselves either join India or Pakistan. Pakistan rejects India's claims to the state under the Instrument of Accession signed by King Hari Singh, as it was done under India's coercion. Pakistan also contends that it has every right to call for self-determination, not only because it is mandated by the UNSC resolutions, but also because it is being demanded by the Kashmiri Muslims through their frequent upris-ings bracing India's brutal oppression. Pakistan claims that it is giving the Kashmiris only moral and diplomatic support and does not send terrorists across the borders, and India accuses it falsely of doing so. Sheikh Abdullah might have accepted the J&K accession to India, but Sardar Abdul Qayyum, the leader of the J&K Muslim Conference (J&KMC), who later became the president and prime minister of Azad Kashmir, does not favor its integration with India, as he also represents the Indian J&K. Furthermore, the current president and prime minister of POK, Sardar Muhammad Masood Khan and Raja Farooq Haider, respectively, also support self-determination for the people of J&K. The Simla accords of 1972, under which Pakistan had agreed to resolve the Kashmir issue bilaterally without UN intervention, was imposed by Indira Gandhi on Pakistan's then Prime Minister Bhutto after India had defeated Pakistan in the 1971 Bangladesh war. Pakistan dismisses India's criticism of its divisive politics by challenging India that it cannot give a holier-than-thou-art posture, because the Muslims who account for 14% percent of India's population continue to experience discrimination and communal riots and assaults incited especially by the Rashtriya Sway-amsevak Sangh (RSS), which fathered Modi's BJP, and the Vishva Hindu Parishad (VHP), and who seek to establish a Hindu Rashtra (Hindu state) on the doctrine of Hindutva (Hindu cultural domination), despite the fact that India had declared itself a secular democracy under its constitution. The destruction of the Babri Mosque in Ayodhya in 1992 by the RSS and the assaults on Muslims in 2001 in the state of Gujarat under Modi as chief minister in which nearly 1,000 Muslims were killed, and other occasional attacks on Muslims, including violence against them and Dalits lately in the name of cow protection laws, all negate the belief that the principles of pluralism and tolerance are being observed and practiced by India.

Pakistan's ruling-elites' hostility towards India remains strong

As Dr. Stephen Cohen notes, the Pakistani ruling elite, also known as the Establishment, comprising business community, journalists, editors, media experts, a few academics and members of think tanks, see India as the chief threat to Pakistan. The elite see armed forces as central to its defense and as such, they deserve a priority position in determining political issues and in the allocation of state resources. For this elite, Kashmir is an impor-tant issue not only because of its strategic importance, but also because of India's malevolence on the issue, and pursuing the cause of Kashmiris with the ultimate goal of incorporating them to Pakistan would fulfill the princi-ple of two-nation theory. In addition, the elite also see the Pakistan army as a model for the rest of Pakistan, as it is seen as selfless, disciplined, obedient and competent and, therefore, its denigration is not to be allowed.[117] In contrast to these hostile attitudes of the Pakistan elites towards India, Minhaz Merchant observes, the Indian elites have succumbed to a Pakistan-funded subverting project in terms of developing positive perceptions of Pakistani elites. He identifies Indian the elites as consisting of film makers, artists, writers, the opposition party politicians and former diplomats who are duped into inviting Pakistani human rights activists, TV anchors, retired army officers and guest speakers to put forth Pakistan's point of view and thus win over a significant section of opinion makers in India. Merchant characterizes these tactics by Pakistan as the wiles of the ISI.[118]

The Pak military seeks conflict to maintain its political dominance

The Pakistan military enjoys a preeminent status as protector of Pakistan against the threat from its nemesis India, although the wars and crises against India have been of the Pakistan military's own making at a huge cost for Pakistanis. The military is the *de facto* controller of Pakistan's foreign and military policy, although it should be the prerogative of the civilian government under the 1973 constitution. No policy initiative taken by civilian government towards India sees the light of day without the military's imprimatur. Whenever the civilian government takes a peace initiative on the Kashmir issue with India, the military invariably intervenes to stymie it by provoking a terrorist attack against India or triggering a crisis. Although under the 1973 constitution, the civilian government's supremacy is affirmed over the military, and under its Article 245, it is a "high treason" for any attempt by the military to abrogate and subvert the constitution "by the use of force or show of force or by other unconstitutional means,"[119] the military has ignored this prohibition and seized power through military coup in 1977 and 1999, and continues to intervene in politics, sometimes supported and welcomed by politicians as part of their revenge politics against their opponents. The Pakistani military ruled the country directly for more than half of its existence, and even when democracy is restored, the civilian leadership owes its survival to the whims of the military. A case in point is the removal of Sharif for the third time, on July 28, 2016, this time by the Supreme Court on the recommendations of a Joint Investigation Team (JIT) for his alleged involvement in the Panama Papers scandal. Sharif was barred for life from political participation. As noted earlier, Sharif's Minister for Petroleum and Natural resources Shahid Abbas had succeeded him as an interim prime minister. The court's summary dismissal of Sharif without a trial is called a "judicial coup." This removal is attributed to the military's alleged influence on the politicized court. It is the current Prime Minister Imran Khan who had sued Sharif before the court on corruption charges. Sharif is the second prime minister to be dismissed by the Supreme Court after Yousuf Raja Gilani.[120] In October, Sharif, his daughter Maryam and her husband Muhammad Safdar were indicted for their alleged illegal ownership of an apartment complex in London while they visited Begum Kulsoom Sharif, who was undergoing cancer treatment. Sharif and his daughter and her husband were subsequently convicted in July 2018 by an anti-corruption court and sentenced to serve ten-year and seven-year jail sentences, respectively, and each pay $10.5 and $2.6 million. Upon their arrival from London, the three were jailed. But on September 11, following Begum Kulsoom's death, they were temporarily released to attend her funeral and memorial both in London and Lahore. But on upon their appeal, a two-panel Islamabad High Court headed by judge Athar Minallah suspended their jail sentences and ordered their release by saying that the National Accountability Bureau (NAB) has failed to prove a link between Sharif and the apartments in London. The court said their convictions still stand until their appeal is heard and disposed of.[121] Sharif, perhaps, would not have paid this humiliating price if he had not defied the military and had been in its good graces. In early October, Sharif's brother, Shahbaz Sharif, the former chief minister of Punjab and the current opposition leader in the National Assembly, was also detained by the NAB on allegations of his illegal award of a contract of Ashiana-i-Iqbal housing scheme.[122] It is ironic that the NAB could have convicted and imprisoned the country's former prime minister when its country is ranked as the third most corrupt in the world according to 2018 Best Countries rankings.[123] Transparency International has also placed Pakistan at the ranking of 117 out of 180 countries in the Corruption Perception Index of 2017.[124] Of course, the corruption is not only Pakistan's problem but is also a third world problem.

Prime Minister Khan is considered to be pro-military. The military played a pivotal role in helping Khan win victory by manipulating the elections in his favor by encouraging defection of politicians to join his party oath by using the tactics of intimidation and persuasion. As Dr. Harsh Pant notes, Khan's victory was foretold, as the military had "shaped the battlefield in Khan's favor" and made it clear to the "civilians that anyone who would dare to cross swords with it would end up languishing in jail like Prime Minister Nawaz Sharif." Pant further notes, after his victory, in his pledge to make a Naya (new) Pakistan, Khan took positions on Afghanistan Taliban, Kashmir, militant groups like the LET in sync with the military's, and Khan's position on India would not be different.[125] Christine Fair also expresses similar views on the Pakistan military and Khan. She writes, "the army resolved to have Khan elected as prime minister" and they are "destined to work together as it needed an ally with which to vanquish its *bête noir*" Sharif, and his party Pakistan Muslim League (Nawaz), and Bhutto's PPP.

She notes, "Not only was the outcome of this election pre-ordained, so are the consequences. Pakistanis will soon discover – sooner than later – that Imran Khan will not be different than their political masters. For international partners, it will be business as usual."[126] M. K. Narayanan, the former National Security Advisor to former Prime Minister Singh, cautions India that it should have more than a tinge of realism in dealing with Khan while welcoming for improved relations with Pakistan. He writes that the Pakistan "deep state" (establishment – military) has played a significant role Khan's election. And over the years "it has co-opted some of the key levers of power, not excluding the judiciary, to maintain its stranglehold on Pakistan," and Khan has little room to manoeuver (to) adopt an path that lead to eventual success, and therefore, to all intents and purposes, (Khan), it appears to be a prisoner the of the "deep state" Narayanan cautions "India would do well to realize this at the beginning of his tenure as prime minister. It is much better than being lulled into a false sense of complacency."[127] If ever Khan crosses military's redlines in seeking peace with India, he is likely to face the same fate as that of Sharif and Bhutto. Unless the military is stripped of its prerogative of making foreign and defense policy, a civilian government might find it difficult to adopt an independent policy of its own in dealing with India. Kashmir is Pakistan's military's fulcrum, not Pakistanis' as a whole. For instance, based on interviews he conducted, Dr. Robert Wirsing notes, he did not find any interest in Kashmir among the people in the provinces of Baluchistan, Sindh, Khyber-Pakhtunkhwa, and the southern part of Punjab, and has found interest only in urban Punjab, especially in the city of Lahore, settled by ethnic Kashmiris, dominated by Islamic fundamentalist groups and also the center of the legal profession, civil service and the military. Wirsing further notes that he has found the military, along with the ISI, as being more than *a primus Interprets* and needs its consent and approval to resolve the Kashmir issue.[128] The military firmly believes that based on the two-nation theory, Kashmir, being a predominantly a Muslim state, should go to Pakistan. It feels that there should be no peace or compromise, although it is an unrealistic dream to achieve in light of the reasons we have cited earlier that explain why India may never concede their demand. However, the military spends nearly 3.5% to 4% of Pakistan's GDP to build both its conventional and nuclear forces so as to confront India over Kashmir. Because of this, Pakistan's military's uncompromising stance, the civilian leadership in Pakistan has not been able to shape and determine Kashmir policy. It is no wonder that on May 25, 1999, in a speech given at the Woodrow Wilson International Center, late Prime Minister Benazir Bhutto said that she had regretted having had adopted a hawkish policy on Kashmir and eschewing dialogue with India, only to pander to the huge Punjab constituency in Pakistan and the hawkish elements within the military who are against any let up on Kashmir.[129] Rattled by global isolation following the Uri terror attack, as reported by the news daily *Dawn*'s reporter Cyril Almeida, on October 6, 2016, Prime Minister Sharif and his officials, in an extraordinary exchange, confronted the army official and asked them to take "visible action" against the JEM and other terrorist groups. The officials asked the military-led intelligence agencies not to interfere with law enforcement acts against the banned militant groups, fresh attempts be made to investigate Pathankot, and restart the stalled Mumbai attacks-related trials at the Rawalpindi anti-terrorism court. This call by the Sharif government resulted a rift between Sharif and the army. But the prime minister's office said the report of the rift was misleading and called it "fiction and fabrication."[130] Upset by the release of a report of the rift, then army chief General Raheel Sharif presided over the meeting of Corps Commanders Conference at the general headquarters in Rawalpindi and expressed serious concern over the story of rift as a breach of national security. Reporter Almeida was later banned from leaving the country.[131] In October 2016, in a strong editorial, the newspaper *The Nation*, which is considered close to government as well as the military establishment, asked why they do not act against Azhar of JEM and Saeed of LET, who are a danger to the country's national security.[132] In an editorial in *Dawn*, in response to the army's criticism of the paper for reporting about the civilian government-army rift, it courageously said Pakistan has "very little or no tradition of holding its armed forces accountable."[133] Although the new army chief Qamar Javed Bajwa is considered professional and apolitical and apparently considers Islamic extremism as a bigger threat than India to Pakistan, one wonders if the hawkish elements in the military will give up its use of terrorism as its policy instrument. The military has divided the terrorists into two groups. For example, the Pakistan military considers groups such as JEM and LET, which are fighting India, and those such as the Afghan Taliban and the Haqqani network which are fighting the Afghan government, "good terrorists"; those fighting Pakistan, however, such as the Pakistani Taliban, Tehrik-I-Taliban Pakistan, TTP), Lashkar-e-Jhangvi (LET), and other terror outfits, it considers "bad" terrorists. In May 2017, Pakistan finally admitted that Saeed of LET was spreading terrorism and put him under house arrest.[134] Saeed, who was the mastermind of the 2008 Mumbai terrorist attacks, until recently was allowed to roam around freely and spew Indian hate propaganda. Surprisingly, he was allowed to form his political party and contest in the recently held July 2018 parliamentary elections. India's efforts to have the UNSC designate Azhar as a terrorist under the 2009 UNSC resolution number 1267 has been blocked by China on behalf of Pakistan, to India's dismay.[135]

The Pakistani military–security establishment does not want to see Azhar declared as terrorist, because, as Raj Verma points out, it finds the Azhar as a valuable person in pursuit of its policy goals towards India as he is an Islamic ideologue, an excellent orator and a brilliant recruiter of Jihadists engaging in an array of Jihadist activities, besides being extremely popular among the anti-India Jihadist outfits.[136]

Its economic interests also prompts the military to keep the conflict aflame as it can deflect the public attention from holding it accountable. In her penetrating work, titled *Military Inc: Inside Pakistan's Military Economy* (2007), Dr. Ayesha Siddiqa describes the military's control of a wide range of its interests worth more than $12 billion.[137] According to her, the military runs five giant conglomerates known as "welfare foundations," under which thousands of businesses, ranging from street corner patrol pumps to sprawling industrial plants, bakeries, banks, insurance companies and universities are usually fronted by civilian employees. Siddiqa estimates that the military controls nearly one-third of all manufacturing. These businesses, Siddiqa points out, benefits primarily the upper echelons of the military such as generals, with little transparency in how these profits are spent, and it spurns the parliament's demands to account for the public monies they spend. She also notes that the military businesses thrive as they get state subsidies in the form of free land and government loans to bail them out when they run into trouble. This pursuit of economic interests is another reason why the military would like to perpetuate the Kashmir conflict. As Sharif had sought to engage India in the peace process, the military hobbled him by stepping up cross-border terrorism against India. Besides, the military has been against Sharif's leadership since the 1990s.[138]

Persistent mutual distrust between the two countries

The partition also that ensued, causing horrendous bloodshed between the Hindus/Sikhs and Muslims and resulting in the death of nearly one million people as they cross-migrated from one side to another of the new border followed by frequent wars and crises over Kashmir, engendered a deep distrust and ill will between India and Pakistan.

The age-old, stubborn distrust that exists between India and Pakistan has hamstrung the peace process over the Kashmir conflict. As Khushwant Singh, in his novel *Train to Pakistan* (1956), describes, the horrific experience as a result of senseless bloodshed, and the displacement that ensued laid the foundation for India-Pakistan distrust.[139] While many Pakistanis led by Jinnah believed in the religion-based two-nation theory, most Indians did not. As such, the Jan Sangh Party (it later changed its name to the BJP) did not believe in the two-nation principle and, therefore, advocated for quite some time for the reunification of mother India with Pakistan. This stance created suspicion among the Pakistanis about India's intensions with respect to Pakistan's integrity and independence. The dismemberment of the country into Pakistan and Bangladesh in 1971 is blamed on India's perfidious motives and its machinations to Pakistan's dismemberment. Pakistani novelist Mohammed Hanif characterizes Indian and Pakistan on and off talks as "dialogue of the deaf" because, as he observes, India accuses Pakistan of sponsoring terrorism in India, while Pakistan accuses India of sponsoring terrorism in Pakistan's province of Baluchistan and of bad manners. Hanif further notes that India is upset that those who were involved in the Mumbai 2008 attacks, including its mastermind Hafiz Saeed, were released on bail and roam around freely, and Saeed addresses anti-Indian rallies. In defense, Pakistan points to its killings of hundreds of suspected terrorists and reminds India that 60,000 of its people have been killed by terrorists. But India responds by saying, "you are killing the terrorists who are killing Pakistanis while protecting the terrorists who kill Indians." Hanif cites some of the stereotypes that India and Pakistan have about each other. For example, "India thinks Pakistan's aging terrorism addict that keeps hitting the world for loose change so it get its next fix. Pakistan thinks, India is an old uncle who has come into some money late in life but does not know how to dress. India says, Pakistan is the pesky kid who is always picking a fight in the neighborhood. Pakistan says, India is the real bully. . . . Go ask the Kashmiris. India says, no one should ask the Kashmiris anything because Pakistan has poisoned their minds." Hanif concludes that "because of these mutual accusations and stereotypes, for 70 years three generations of Indians and Pakistanis have lived with war or the imminent threat of war, and maybe it is time for India and Pakistan to do away with the pretense that they want peace. Hundreds of miles of barbed wires on the border, countless search lights and miles-long visa forms have not made us secure about each other."[140] Therefore, it is no wonder that opinion polls indicate very unfavorable views of each other between the two nations. For example, in a survey conducted by the Pew Research Center in 2011, only 14% of Pakistanis saw India in a positive light while 75% saw it negatively, and 74% considered India as a serious threat to their country. A majority of Pakistanis considered India as a more serious threat to their country than al Qaeda. Indians' view of Pakistan was equally negative. Only 14% of them gave Pakistan a favorable rating while 65% of them gave a negative opinion. However, 70% of Pakistanis and 74% of Indians wanted improved relations between them. Seventy percent of Pakistanis considered Kashmir a big problem and said it was the crux of tensions between the two countries.[141] In another poll conducted by the Lowy Institute in 2013, 94% of Indians saw Pakistan as a threat, citing terrorism as a major reason. Even so, 89% of them agreed that ordinary people in both countries want peace and 87% agreed that a big improvement in India-Pakistan relations required courageous leadership on both sides, and 76% agreed that India should take the initiative.[142] Malik Siraj Akbar, a Pakistani columnist, notes that Pakistan is hurting itself for blaming India for all its problems. Akbar points out,

> blaming India for bad governance inside Pakistan is as old as the country's creation in 1947, and with the passage of time, this practice of blaming India has worked so well in the country's politics that the civilian, military, and religious leaders all use it to hide their failures and externalize the blame. However, this approach is tremendously hurting the ordinary people in Pakistan.[143]

To perpetuate the distrust and negative views of India and its people, Pakistani governments played a prominent role in indoctrinating their people through their biased textbooks and history. For example, in 2011, the US Commission on International Religious Freedom (USCIRF) reviewed 100 textbooks from grades 1 to 10 from Pakistan's four provinces; visited 37 public schools and 19 madrasas; and interviewed 277 teachers and students. Based on these interviews and examination of the books, the commission prepared a report. It indicates that there is a systematic negative portrayal of minorities, especially Hindus, and notes that "Hindus are repeatedly described as extremists and eternal enemies of Islam and whose culture and society is based on injustice and cruelty, while Islam delivers a message of peace and brotherhood, concepts alien to the Hindus." The books, the report notes, makes "very little reference to the role played by Hindus, Sikhs and Christians in the cultural, military, and civic life of Pakistan" and exonerate or glorify Islamic civilization and denigrate civilizations of religious minorities.[144] In 2016, the Pakistani *Herald* invited writers and commentators well versed in history to share their views about what is taught in Pakistani textbooks. They said that a blatant lie is taught about Pakistan's history about Muslims, India and Hindus.[145] But the Pakistani government has not made any attempt so far to reform its curriculum to deal with these historic distortions. This is not the case for Indian textbooks, which the BJP seeks to revise but is being resisted by Indian scholars and writers.

Although the issues discussed above such as cross-border terrorism, mutual claims to the state of J&K, and Pakistan military's desire to keep the conflict aflame in order to maintain its dominance of Pakistan'politics, offer some explanations for the persistence of the Kashmir conflict, and which defy solution, as recognized by the Modi government recently, it cannot afford to, from not embarking on peace process with Pakistan to resolve the conflict. And given the fact the Modi government's military approach has failed to put down the insurgency in the Valley, and given the fact that this approach has damaged India's image as a democracy, besides causing loss of life and loss to its treasury, the Modi government may have to reevaluate its current policy on the insurgency. Even with the ongoing insurgency, it is imperative that the composite dialogue be revived with ardent commitment to resolve the Kashmir conflict once and for all by bringing all the stakeholders representing the separatists, the insurgency leaders in the Valley, the Hindus of Jammu, the Buddhists of Ladakh, the representatives of the POK, and the main protagonist Pakistan. A highly respected and seasoned diplomat who is an expert on Kashmir and Pakistan, aided by experts on the conflict, should be the center's interlocutor to deal with such a complex issue like Kashmir. The government also ought to take into its confidence opposition political parties who all desire resolution of this conflict. Besides, the center also has to create proper atmospherics conducive to facilitating talks by taking measures such as repealing the much-hated AFSPA and by pledging to conduct a speedy trial of those security forces who have been implicated in human rights abuses. The center may have to withdraw the military forces and use them primarily to protect the borders and the country from cross-border terrorism and Pakistan's threats, instead of using them to deal with domestic insurgencies. It should be the responsibility of local police and the paramilitary forces to deal with such internal insurgency. The Indian military is non-political and enjoys great respect and admiration among the Indian people, and that should be maintained by not using them to deal with internal insurgencies to the extent possible. By taking these measures, the Modi government could gain the confidence of the separatists and the insurgents and persuade them to come to the table. With respect to Baluchi separatists, the Modi government should disavow its support and pledge its commitment to Pakistan's national integrity so as to avoid any of its misgivings of India's intentions. C. Raja Mohan has suggested a number of recommendations for the Modi government to consider in reviving the peace process with Pakistan. Some of those recommendations include exploring opening up a channel of communication with the Pakistan army; resisting pressure from the media to suspend the peace process at the first setback; drawing the opposition parties into the peace process; and liberalizing the visa regime to promote exchanges with Pakistanis.[146] Modi is the right leader to address this long-festering problem because he is a Hindu nationalist who has earned a mandate by winning a landslide victory in the 2014 parliamentary elections, although his party is perceived to be anti-Muslim and anti-minority. As noted earlier, some of his party members have committed attacks, including the killing of Muslims and Dalits for their alleged killing of cows, in the name of cow protection. These assaults have created a credibility problem for Modi's government in dealing with Kashmir, which is predominantly Muslim. Modi has to disabuse the people of these perceptions by punishing those of his party members who indulge in such criminal behavior and by genuinely committing himself to the peace process. Like the conservative Republican President Nixon having opened to communist China in 1972, Modi, as a Hindu nationalist leader who enjoys a great deal of credibility among the Hindu nationalist parties and groups, could achieve a peace deal with Kashmiris and Pakistanis that the predominantly Hindu Indians would be likely to accept. But what are the alternative solutions and which one of them can a viable solution to the conflict?

Alternative solutions, and the viable one to resolve the conflict

Professor Raju Thomas offers the following alternative solutions to resolve the conflict and discusses them in in detail in terms of their pros and cons. They are as follows:

1   Maintain the territorial status quo in Kashmir.
2   Secure Kashmir's accession to Pakistan.
3   Create an independent Kashmir.
4   Secure a "Trieste" solution (like the one reached between Yugoslavia and Italy) through a territorial transfer of the Valley of Kashmir to Pakistan.
5   Manipulate a "Tibetan" solution by transforming the demographics in Kashmir.
6   Generate an exodus of Kashmiri Muslims into Pakistan.
7   Achieve joint Indo-Pakistani control over Kashmir.
8   Foster a subcontinent of several independent states.
9   Promote a decentralized subcontinental confederation of several autonomous states.[147]

Among the above alternative solutions suggested by Professor Thomas, it is safe to assume that solutions 2–9 are impractical or unfeasible, as none of the principal parties to the conflict are likely to accept any one of them. The solution perhaps, which both India and Pakistan including the Kashmiris in the Valley, as well as those in POK could accept, is the first solution, that is maintaining the current status quo along the LOC. India may accept the LOC as the international border, whereby it will retain its part of Kashmir and Pakistan retains its part – the POK. The Kashmiris are likely to be satisfied too, if full autonomy, as had been agreed to under the Instrument of Accession and granted to the people of J&K under Article 370, is restored. The Kashmiri Muslims in the Valley may have to accept this deal, given the fact the Pandits in the Valley, and the people in the Jammu and Ladakh regions, want to be part of India. The Kashmiris in POK may also accept being part of Pakistan if a similar status of autonomy under their own constitution is granted to them. According to D. P. Dhar, advisor to the late Prime Minister Indira Gandhi who had attended the Simla conference held in 1972, the late Prime Minister Zulfiqar Ali Bhutto reportedly told Gandhi, "the Line of Control will become the border, that over the years, he would be able to convince the people what is India's is India's and what is ours is ours."[148] As noted earlier, General Musharraf also offered a proposal along the same lines in 2003–4. Even the Pakistan military, which has been intransigent all these years on this conflict, may come around to supporting peace talks, given the fact that it is coming under severe pressure from the Trump administration and US congress for its alleged support of terrorism. For example, in his visit to New Delhi on October 26, 2017, the former US Secretary of State Rex Tillerson warned Pakistan that terror safe havens would not be tolerated and that it was harboring too many terror organizations. In Islamabad, the secretary repeated the same warning when he met with Prime Minister Abbasi. He told Abbasi that he should act against terror or "we will get it done."[149] The Trump administration has cut off economic and military aid to the tune of one billion dollars as punishment for Pakistan's continued alleged support for the Afghan Taliban. Pakistan may not want to be isolated and become a pariah internationally anymore. The Pakistan military perhaps realizes that its support for terrorism in pursuit of its short-term interests has not only isolated the country, but has also given the country a reputation as a center of terrorism. Currently, as of this writing, Khan's government is facing an economic crisis with a mounting balance of payments problem. The government has approached the International Monetary Fund (IMF) reportedly for a $12 billion loan to help bail it out of this crisis. Pakistani Finance Minister Asad Umar has indicated that he would soon begin talks with the IMF. But addressing a news conference at the IMF and World Bank annual meeting in Bali, Indonesia, the IMF's economist Maurice Obstfeld cautioned Pakistan that it should be ready to undertake structural reforms and refrain from taking excessive loans from China, which is investing close to $60 billion in Pakistan as part of CPEC projects under Chinese One Belt One Road Initiative. The IMF loans are given under certain conditions. US Secretary of State Mike Pompeo disfavors IMF loans to Pakistan, saying there was "no rationale" to bail out Pakistan to pay Chinese loans to Pakistan.[150]

Unlike his predecessors, Pakistan's current army chief General Bajwa, who knows India's current army chief Rawat (they both served together in UN peacekeeping operation in the Republic of Congo in the 1990s), appears to be interested resuming in genuine peace talks with India. For instance, appearing before Pakistan's senate in December 2017, General Bajwa said, "We can resolve issues with India through talks instead of war.

In this situation if the government decides to hold talks with India, then the army would back the government."[151] He voiced a similar position in April 2018 while speaking during a passing out parade of Pakistan military academy in April 2018. He said, "it is our sincere belief that the route to peaceful resolution of Pak-India disputes – including the core issue of Kashmir – runs through comprehensive and meaningful dialogue" and a call for peace talks in no sense should be considered a sign of weakness on the part of Pakistan.[152] The Hurriyat leader Mirwaiz Farooq, in an article published on September 30, 2018, in *Dawn.com*, repeated his call on India for a dialogue with Pakistan as the only way to resolve the Kashmir conflict while also accusing India of its many atrocities in the Valley and how much of a price both counties are paying by not addressing their peoples' needs as they are engaged in an arms race due to this conflict.[153] Farooq writes, "We Kashmiris know that our salvation lies in shift in outlook and policy. We also know that this shift is possible only through dialogue – dialogue as we all understand is currently the most civilized and humane way to resolve conflicts." He points out,

> the current backtracking and hardening of position by the government of India is directly linked to its (2019) general elections. The ruling BJP cannot afford to be seen soft on "terrorism" – a frightening bogey which has been created and which in India is now synonymous with Pakistan. [. . .] because of this conflict, trade potential which stands at $37 billion between India and Pakistan today is only $2 billion, and that UN Human Development Index (HDI) of 2017 ranks India number 136 and Pakistan 150 while they have distinguished themselves by out-running each other in the arms race [according to Stockholm International Peace Research Institute-SIPRI 2017 data, India and Pakistan spend 2.5 and 3.5 percent of their GDP on military respectively] by draining their economies.

He describes Kashmir as human tragedy, and accuses India for this tragedy and denounces its repression of the people in the Valley. He writes,

> an outcome of deception and betrayal by successive governments in India, leading to families torn apart, swelling graveyards, repression and blindness, disappearance, and sexual crimes – the entire gamut of human rights abuse and severe injustice. It is the complete moral and political failure of the Indian state. To occupy people and their land against their will. To exert control by fostering draconian laws to facilitate unabated killings by its military apparatus, crushing democratic rights and political dissent, restricting free speech, incarcerating,

torturing and continuing to keep hundreds of thousands of military forces deployed for decades on end.

As the Modi government realizes, "guns and abuses" will not resolve the conflict. Its military policy in the Valley will not bring end to the militancy. The government should be willing to address the fundamental causes that have triggered this insurgency in the Valley since the late 1980s. India cannot blame Pakistan entirely for the insurgency, although as we have noted earlier, it does foster terrorism through its funding and training of the Kashmiri militants, as well as by encouraging cross-border infiltration. The Modi government should know that repression only further alienates the Kashmiris instead of winning them over. In his study of the situation in Kashmir, Jeffrey Gettleman of *The New York Times* (August 1, 2018) describes it as "blood and grief in an intimate war."[154] Because of repression being perpetrated by the Indian security forces, a large majority of Kashmiris support the militant youth and they "hate India" and do not want to be part of India. They favor independence (Azadi) as they feel alienated from India. He notes, while protests against India have grown in number and size, the armed militancy has become small – around 250 operating in Kashmir down from thousands a decade ago, and points out that according to police officials, of these 250, only 50 came from Pakistan and have never left the Valley. Pakistan is not providing as much support as it used to. To put down this militancy of 250 armed men, Gettleman notes, 250,000 Indian army soldiers, border guards, police officers and police reserves are stationed in the Valley, outnumbering the militants 1,000 to one. The Modi government may have to reexamine whether it needs so many security forces not to put down the militancy domestically, especially military soldiers whose job is to protect borders and its people from external threats. The Modi government may have to reciprocate the calls from Pakistani leaders for dialogue by agreeing to hold talks to end the conflict instead of insisting on Pakistan ending its support for terrorism as a condition to revive the dialogue. By agreeing to talks, the Modi government will have an opportunity to test the sincerity of Pakistani leaders who say they seek to end the conflict for the long-term interests of both countries. As noted earlier, given its isolation, mounting economic crisis and rising terrorism internally, and with a separatist movement in Baluchistan, Pakistan may be compelled to reevaluate its support for the Kashmiri militancy and seek a genuine peace with India. Pakistan today has become a failing state. Modi may want to emulate the model set by US President Jimmy Carter, who had helped to end the long-running conflict between Egypt and Israel by convincing both late President Anwar Sadat and Prime Minister Menachem Begin to sign the Camp David accords at a thirteen-day summit held at Camp David in September 1978. Carter was subsequently awarded the Nobel Peace Prize for this agreement, as were Sadat and Begin. The Kashmir conflict has become an albatross around India's neck since 1947. If India and Pakistan can achieve peace over Kashmir, both can prosper immensely by devoting their scarce resources and talents for the common weal of their peoples by ameliorating their peoples' economic, social, educational, health and housing problems. India and Pakistan are poor countries. For example, according to a 2011 survey, the poverty levels of India and Pakistan stood at 29.5%.[155] India and Pakistan cannot to afford to allocate 2.5% and 3.5% percent of their GDP, respectively, for their militaries, thus engaging in an arms race when they have so many urgent problems to address. It is, therefore, high time that India and Pakistan meet and resolve the Kashmir conflict. Peace between India and Pakistan is imperative.

Conclusion

We have discussed the Indo-Pakistan conflict over Kashmir by focusing on the origins of the conflict, the wars and the crises that took place between India and Pakistan since 1947 to the present. For instance, on the origins of the conflict, as we have discussed, the Indian troops intervened on behalf of the state of J&K only after King Hari Singh had signed the Instrument of Accession to defend the state against Pakistan's invasion. However, even before the whole state was liberated, Prime Minister Nehru took the issue to the UN to file a complaint against Pakistan for its aggression. At the same time, Nehru pledged to hold a plebiscite in the state once the Pakistani troops were withdrawn from the occupied Kashmir. It was his pledge that had prompted the UN to attempt to conduct a plebiscite, but it was unsuccessful, as India and Pakistan disagreed by offering their own conditions and interpretations of UNSC resolutions. This stalemate between India and Pakistan subsequently led to wars in 1965, 1971 and 1998, excluding other crises. If Nehru had conducted the promised plebiscite in the 1950s and 1960s, because much good will existed among the Kashmiris at that time, it is safe to assume that a majority of Kashmiris might have opted for India, and consequently the Indo-Pakistan conflict might have ended. But because Nehru did not hold the plebiscite, the conflict persists until today. We have presented some plausible factors for the continued conflict, such as mutual claims to the state, the Pakistani elite's hostile attitude towards India, the Pakistani military's interest in keeping the conflict aflame as a vehicle to maintain its privileges and perks, and the mistrust and misperceptions that exist between India and Pakistan. We have pointed out that it was India's nonchalant attitude in not respecting the state's autonomy as guaranteed under Article 370, and its heavy-handed and interventionist patterns of behavior towards the Kashmiris, especially under Indira Gandhi and her son Rajiv that led to an alienation of a large segment of the Kashmiri population and which eventually led to insurgency in late 1980s. The iron-fisted approach in the handling of the militants and their supporters further aggravated the situation by intensifying Kashmiri Muslims' anger and hostility towards India. In the wake of this indigenous uprising, the Pakistani military seized the opportunity to cash in on the troubled waters by supporting and fostering the insurgency to brow beat India. However, under the Vajpayee and Singh governments, with their conciliatory approach, the insurgency subsided, and a relative calm was witnessed in the Valley, accompanied by an Indo-Pak agreement to launch a composite dialogue, which also included the Kashmir issue for discussion for the first time. But the dialogue came to a screeching halt when ten Pakistani terrorists attacked the city of Mumbai, killing and wounding hundreds of civilians, and Pakistan was subsequently reluctant to try and punish the conspirators for this heinous crime. But with the killing of Hizbul Mujahideen leader Wani in July 2016, the insurgency was again revived, and the Modi government's maximalist military policy to put down the insurgency, as it lately has acknowledged, has failed to end it as Pakistan continues to support the insurgency. We point out that given current Pakistan's increasing levels of global isolation and its mounting economic problems followed by the Khan government's call for dialogue and supported openly its Chief of Army of Pakistan for the first time, it is the propitious time for the Modi government to seize this opportunity and reciprocate Pakistan's call for dialogue with consent to revive it to resolve the Kashmir issue. We suggest that the Modi government should consider appointing a seasoned and well-respected expert diplomat to lead the dialogue by inviting in to the negotiating table all stakeholders in the conflict and resolve it once and for all. We believe Modi, a Hindu nationalist, is the right leader to resolve the conflict, because he enjoys credibility among a wide segment of the Indian population. As Sandeep Bhardwaj points out, it is high time that the Modi government abandons its "brinkmanship" policy and demonstrates "statesmanship" by replacing its maximalist policy with a moderate and conciliatory one to resolve the Kashmir problem.[156] It is amazing to note that the new governor Malik has indicated on October 24, 2018, that he will not engage in talks with the Kashmiri regional parties – NC, PDP and the separatist Hurriyat leaders unless they give up on demanding for Pakistan's involvement as a condition for their joining the talks with India. Malik warned that Kashmiri leaders

> have no right to talk about India-Pakistan peace talks. It is between governments of the two nations as being neighbors makes it obvious

that talks will happen for sure. But political parties bringing up the issue of Pakistan into dialogue process was neither acceptable to us then, nor will it be now.

In response, Mehbooba Mufti of the PDP said she will pitch for India-Pakistan dialogue, saying the relations have bearing on Kashmir, and Hurriyat leader Mirwaiz Farooq characterized Malik's remark as "illiteracy on Kashmir."[157] Malik's statement appears to show his naiveté on the issue when Pakistan is the principal protagonist to this conflict. We have identified some alternative solutions to the conflict, and suggest the one – the LOC as being the international boundary which parties to the conflict might accept if the Kashmiris on either side of the LOC were given full autonomy with freedom to interact with each other economically, culturally and socially. Even though India claims the entire J&K and even though Pakistan demands self-determination, they are not unrealistic claims and demands. For India could never acquire the POK, and neither can Pakistan ever expect India to agree to self-determination, as circumstances in the Valley have changed today. For instance, as Dr. Damodar Sar Desai notes, India has argued that it is perfectly entitled to rely on the principle of doctrine of *rebus sic stantibus* in not fulfilling its previous pledge. For, under this doctrine, a state is exonerated from its obligation from its international commitment if there is a vital change in the circumstances that had existed at the time the obligation was undertaken.[158] Pakistan and Kashmiri militants have to recognize that fact.

India and Pakistan face multiple problems, such as poverty, illiteracy, lack of access to health care, housing and infrastructure, and therefore they cannot afford to devote their scarce resources to engage in an arms race triggered by this conflict. The resolution of this festering conflict will result in the availability of these resources for better use – to build their societies into prosperous ones as China and other Asian tigers have achieved.

Historically, the Kashmiri Muslims have been docile, secular, tolerant as being Sufi and pro-Indian. In the past, Pakistan had little constituency for it in the Kashmir Valley. But that has changed today as the Kashmiri Muslims have turned anti-Indian, having been alienated because of India's shortsighted and repressive policies. It is therefore incumbent on the Modi government, or whichever government may emerge after the 2019 parliamentary elections, to adopt a genuine conciliatory approach towards the Kashmiri Muslims to win it over to India so that they can accept happily being an integral part of India, and live with respect and dignity as Indian citizens in a secular democratic India. To help transform a multi-religious, multi-ethnic and multi-lingual India into an egalitarian and integrated India, Modi's BJP/RSS may have to abandon its divisive, sectarian doctrine of Hindutva and embrace the principle of Indian culture if there is such a word in

English language. The Hindutva doctrine will not win over Indian Muslims in general and Kashmiri Muslims in particular, who account for the second largest population in the world after Indonesia. Kashmiri Muslims are suspicious of the Modi government's credentials and intentions when its BJP/RSS question the autonomy given them under Articles 370 and 35A of the Indian constitution.

Notes

1 For text of the instrument, see Sumit Ganguly, *Conflict Unending: India-Pakistan Tensions Since 1947* (New York: Columbia University Press, 2001), pp. 150–1.
2 For text of India's complaint to the UN, see ibid., pp. 152–3.
3 For text of the UN resolution of August 13, 1948, see ibid., pp. 158–60.
4 For a detailed discussion about the origins of the Kashmir dispute, the first Indo-Pakistan war and the UN Security Council's attempts to resolve it, see ibid., pp. 15–27; Sisir Gupta, *Kashmir* (New York: Asian Publishing House, 1966), pp. 1–439; Alastair Lamb, *Kashmir* (Hertingfordbury, UK: Roxford Books, 1991), pp. 83–260; Gowher Rizvi, "India, Pakistan, and the Kashmir Problem 1947–1972"; Damodar Sar Desai, "The Organs of Kashmir International, and Legal Status"; and Pervaiz Iqbal Cheema, "Pakistan, India and Kashmir: A Historical Review," in Raju Thomas (ed.), *Perspectives on Kashmir: The Roots of Conflict in South Asia* (Boulder: Westview Press, 1992), pp. 47–118, and Josef Korbel, *Danger in Kashmir* (Princeton: Princeton University, 1966), pp. 73–337.
5 For more details about state's internal political changes, see Rathnam Indurthy, "Kashmir in Indo-Pakistani Relations: Mutual Claims to State as the Causes of the Conflict," *Asian Profile*, February 2002, Vol. 30, No. 1, pp. 39–40.
6 Ganguly, *Conflict Unending*, p. 40.
7 For more details about the war, see ibid., pp. 43–6; Rajesh Kadian, *The Kashmir Tangle* (Boulder: Westview Press, 1993), pp. 62–128, and Mushtaqur Rahman, *Divided Kashmir* (Boulder: Lynn Leimer Publishers, 1999), pp. 110–17.
8 For text of the agreement, see Ganguly, *Conflict Unending*, pp. 162–3.
9 For more detailed discussion about the Bangladeshi people's rebellion and the Indo-Pakistan war, see ibid., pp. 51–74.
10 For text of the agreement, see ibid., pp. 168–9.
11 Indurthy, "Kashmir in Indo-Pakistani Relations," p. 43.
12 For more details of the insurgency, see Sumit Ganguly, "Avoiding War in Kashmir," *Foreign Affairs*, Vol. 69, No. 5 (Winter 1990–91), pp. 57–73; Edward Desmond, "Himalayan Ulster," *The New Review of Books* (March 1991), pp. 24–7, and Anthony Spaeth, "No Peace in the Valley," *Harper's Magazine* (April 1993), pp. 81–7.
13 Ganguly, *Conflict Unending*, pp. 9–94.
14 For detailed description of the abuses by both India and the militants, see Human Rights Watch, "The Human Rights Crisis in Kashmir," New York, 1993, and Kanhya Kaul and M. K. Teng, "Human Rights Violations of Kashmiri Hindus," Thomas (ed.), *Perspectives of Kashmir*, pp. 175–87.

15 For more details about Indian government's approach towards the militancy in the mid-1990s and the responses of some of the militant leaders, see Rathnam Indurthy, "Kashmir Between India and Pakistan: An Intractable Conflict," *The Resurging India*, Vol. 2, No. 1 (January–June 2005), pp. 8–11.
16 Robert Wirsing, "India-Pakistan Relations, and the Problem of Kashmir," *Indian Journal of Politics*, Vol. 32, Nos. 3–4 (July–December 1998), pp. 118–21.
17 Rathnam Indurthy, "India's Nuclear Testing, and the Clinton Administration: From Estrangement to Engagement," *Indian Journal of Politics*, Vol. 36, Nos. 3–4 (July–December 2002), p. 23.
18 Indurthy, "Kashmir Between India and Pakistan," pp. 13–14.
19 For text of the declaration, see Ganguly, *Conflict Unending*, pp. 170–1.
20 The discussion of the war and its resolution is drawn primarily from ibid., pp. 114–21.
21 For details about factors leading to military overthrow or military coup, and Sharif's trial and exile, see Rathnam Indurthy, "Musharraf's Regime in Pakistan: The Praetorianism Faces an Uncertain Future," *The Indian Journal of Political Science*, Vol. 65, No. 2 (April–June 2004), pp. 263–4.
22 "Evidence," *India Today International* (March 13, 2000), p. 23.
23 Ibid., February 26, pp. 26–31, and Navnita Behera, *Demystifying Kashmir* (Washington, DC: Brookings Institution Press, 2006), pp. 145–62.
24 Behera, *Demystifying Kashmir*, p. 53.
25 For details on the failure of Agra talks, see Ganguly, *Conflict Unending*, pp. 135–8.
26 Rathnam Indurthy and Muhammad Haque, "The Kashmir Conflict: Why It Defies Solution," *International Journal on World Peace*, Vol. 37, No. 1 (March 2002), pp. 14–15.
27 Ibid., pp. 16–17.
28 For more details about the composite dialogue, see ibid., pp. 18–21.
29 Steve Coll, "The Back Channel," *The New Yorker*. www.newyorker.com/magazine/2009/03/02/the-back-channel (accessed on 7/15/2015).
30 For more details of India's relations with the Gilani government from March to December 2008, see Indurthy and Haque, "The Kashmir Conflict," pp. 28–30.
31 For more details about the attack, and the response of India and the international community, see ibid., pp. 30–3, and, "@008 the Terrorist," *India Today International* (January 5, 2009), pp. 18–31.
32 For more details about Indo-Pakistan relations, and the dialogue for the period 2009 to 2014, see www.mea.govt.in.portal/foreign relation/pakistan-August 2012.pdf and www.mea.govt.in/portal/foreign relation/pakistan-april 2014/pdf (accessed on 5/2/2016).
33 Kanti Bajpai, "Narendra Modi's Pakistan and China Policy: Assertive Bilateral Diplomacy, Active Coalition Diplomacy," *International Affairs*, Vol. 93, No. 1 (2017), pp. 73.
34 "India Prime Minister Calls Pakistan President to Wish Him Luck Ahead of Cricket World Cup," *The National*. www.thenational.ae/sport/cricket/india-pm-pm-narendra-modi-calls-pakistan-pm (accessed on 5/12/2017).
35 "SAARC Yatra Talks with Pakistan Secretary Constructive," *The Hindu*. www.thehindu.com/news/national/indias-foreign-secretary-s-jaishanker-in-pak (accessed on 5/25/2017).

36 Kanti Bajpai, "Narendra Modi's Pakistan and China Policy," *International Affairs*, Vol. 93, No. 1 (2017), p. 74.

37 "India, Pakistan NSAs Meet in Bangkok," *The Hindu*. www.thehindu. com/news/national/national-security-advisors-ofindia-and-pa (accessed on 5/17/2017).

38 "7 Years After Mumbai Attacks, India, Pakistan Resume Dialogue," *The Hindu*. www.thehindu.com/news/internaional/india-Pakistan-announce-revival-of-ta (accessed on 5/18/2017).

39 "PM Goes to Lahore, Makes a Christmas Date with History," *The Hindu*. www.thehindu.com/news/national/pm-goes-to-lahore-makes-a-Christmas-d (accessed on 5/18/2017).

40 Raja Mohan, "How Prime Minister Modi Can Sustain India's Pakistan Dialogue," *Carnegie India*. https://carnegieindia.org/2016/02/12/how-prime-minister-modi-can-sustain-india-s-pakistan-dialogue-pub-62707, and Bajpai, "Narendra Modi's Pakistan and China Policy," pp. 74–5.

41 Nida Najar, "How Killing of Prominent Separatist Set off Turmoil in Kashmir," *New York Times*, July 15, 2016.

42 "Pakistan Celebrates Independence Day," *The Hindu*. www.thehindu.com/news/international/pakistan-celebrates-independence-Da (accessed on 6/19/2017).

43 "Modi Questions Pak on Rights Abuses in Balochistan, POK," *The Hindu*. www.thehindu.com/news/national/Modi-questions-Pak-on-rights-abuses-in- (accessed on 5/25/2017).

44 "Uri Terror Attack," *The Times of India*. http://times of india.indiatimes.com/uri-terror-attack-indian-army-camp-attacked-in-jammu-and-kashmir-17 killed-19-injured/articleshowprint/54389451.cms (accessed on 9/20/2016).

45 "Those Behind Uri Attack Won't Go Unpunished: Modi," *The Hindu*. www.the hindu.com/news/national/primw-minister-narendra-modi-condemns-uri-terroe-attack/article9120957.ece (accessed on 9/20/2016).

46 "62% of Indians Want Military Might Used to Beat Terror," *The Times of India*. http://timesofindia.indiatimes.com. articleshowprint54413032.cms (accessed on 9/21/2016).

47 "India Exports Software, Pakistan Exports Terror," *The Times of India*. http://time sofindia.indiatimes.com/articleshowprint/54497875.cms (accessed on 10/2/2016).

48 "Uri Attack Could be Reaction to Situation in Kashmir," *The Times of India*. http://timesofindia.indiatimes.comworld/Pakistan/uri-attack-could-be-reaction-to-situation-in-kashmir-nawaz-Sharif/articleshowprint/54494000.cms?null (accessed on 9/25/2016).

49 "Uri Terror Attack: PM Likens Anger to 1965," *The Times of India*. https://timesofindia.indiatimes.com/india/Uri-terror-attack-pm-likens-anger-t-1965-reposes-faith-in-army/articleshowprint/54507391.cms?null (accessed on 10/5/2016).

50 "Surgical Strikes a Message to Pakistan, Escalation Unlikely," *The Times of India*. http://timesofindia.indiatimes.com/surgical strikes-a-message-to-Paki stan-escalation-unlikely-security-experts/articleshowprint/54592059.cms? null, and "Army Surgical Strikes Across LOC," http://timesofindia.india times.com/india/army-surgical-strikes-across-loc-full-statement-by-DGMO-Lt-Gen-ranbir-singh/aticles/howprint/54582733.cms?null (accessed on 9/10/2016).

51 "Pakistan Defence Minister Khawaja Mohammad Asif threatens to Unleash Nukes Against India," *The Times of India.* http://timesofindia.indiatimes. com/india/pakistan-defece-minister-Khwaja-Muhammad-Asif-threatens-to-unleash-nukes-against-india/articleshowprint/54574492.cms?null (accessed on 10/3/2016).

52 "Pakistan Gets US Smackdown for Immature Nuclear Talk," *The Times of India.* http://timesofindia.indiatimes.comindia/Pakistan-gets-US-smackdown-for-immature-nuclear-talk/articleshowprint/54626894.cms?null (accessed on 10/25/2016).

53 Elien Barry, "India Claims Surgical Strikes Across Line of Control in Kashmir," *The New York Times.* www.nytimes.com/2016/09/30/world/asia/Kashmir-india-pakistan.html?r=0 (accessed on 10/3/2016).

54 "At Times, War Becomes Unavoidable, Says PM Narendra Modi," *The Times of India.* https://timesofindia.indiatimes.com/india/At-times-war-becomes-unavoidable-says-PM-Narendra-Modi/articleshow/54803023.cms (accessed on 11/2/2016).

55 "Mother-Ship of Terror," *The Times of India.* http://timesofindia.indiatimes. com/india/Pakistan-mother-ship-terrorism-PM-Nrendra-Modi-tells-BRICS-leaders/articleshowprint/54878345.cms?null (accessed on 11/2/2016).

56 "Pak Envoy Slams India for Trying to Isolate It on Terror," *The Times of India.* http://timesofindia.indiatimes.com/world/Pak-envoy-slams-india-for-trying-to-isolate-it-on-terror/articleshowprint55034802.cms?null (accessed on 11/1/2016).

57 "Pakistan Uses Terrorism as Instrument of State Policy," *The Times of India.* http//timesofindia.indiatimes.com/india//Pakistan-uses-terrorism-as-instrument-of-state-policy-Rajnath/articleshowprint/55040226.cms?null (accessed on 11/3/2016).

58 Smruti Pattanaik, "Cancellation of the SAARC Summit," *The Institute for Defence Studies and Analyses.* http://idsa.in/idsacomments/cancellation-of-the-SARRC-summit_summitsspattanaik_290916 (accessed on 10/20/2016).

59 For more details, see "Blood and Water Can't Flow Together," *Hindustan Times.* www.hindustantimes.com/india-news/blood-and-water-can-t-flow-together-says-modi-at-meeting-on-indus-treaty/story/-4dl.html, and "Indus Waters Treaty," *Firstpost India.* www.firstpost.com/india/indus-water-offensive-can-unspeakable-havoc-for-pakistan-3022158.html (accessed on 10/11/2016).

60 Salman Masood, "Pakistan Sentences Indian Spy to Death for Operating Terrorism Ring," *The New York Times.* www.nytimes.com/2017/04/10/world/asia/pakistan-india-death-sentence-spykulbhushan-y, and "Kulbhishan Jadhav's Death Sentence," http://timesofindia.indiatimes.com/india/kulbhushan-jadhavs-death-sentence-accusations-in-pak-letter-irk-india/articleshowprint/58137743.cms (accessed on 5/20/2017).

61 "International Court of Justice Stays Execution of Kulbhushan Jadhav in Pakistan," *Scroll India.* https://scroll.in/article837137 (accessed on 7/3/2017).

62 "UN Report Slams Opaque Pak Military Courts," *The Times of India.* http:// timesofindia.india.times.com/india/un-report-slams-opaque-pak-military-courts-try-jadhav-loke-caes-says-panel-/articleshowprint56869592.cms?null (accessed on 6/20/ 2017).

63 "Petition in Pakistan Supreme Court Seeks Immediate Execution of Kulbhushan Jadhav," *The Times of India.* http://timesofindia.indiantimes.com/world/Pakistan/petition-supreme-court-seeks-immediate-excution-of-kulbhshan-jadhav/articleshowprint/58878480.coms (accessed on 6/2/2017).

64 For more details about the treatment of protesters, the media and elite reactions, see "100 Days of Unrest in Kashmir," *Scroll India*. http://scroll.in/article819142/100-days-of-unrest-in-kashmir-curfew-pellets-shutd, and "A Cruel April in Kashmir," *The New York Times*. www.nytimes.com/2017/0425/opinion-/a-cruel-april inkshmir-htmal?rref=cllection%2Fti (accessed on 7/2/2017).

65 "Hizbul Mujahideen Chief Zakir Musa Quits After Threatening to Behead Hurriyat Leaders," https://scroll.in/latest/837532/hizbul-commander-zakir-musa-quits-after-group-mem (accessed on 7/5/2017).

66 "Hizbul Mujahideen Terrorist Sabzar Bhat Killed," http://timesofindia.india times.com/india/hizbul-mujahideen-terrorist-sabzar-bhat-killed-curfew-in-parts-of-srinagar-on-Sunday-/articleshowprint/58872836.cms(accessedon6/11/2017).

67 "Pakistani, Saudi Channels Beam into Kashmiri Homes, Stokes Azadi," *The Times of India*. http://timesofindia.inatimes.com/india/Pakistani-saudi-channels-beam-into-kashmiri-homes-stokes-azadi-rage/articleshowprint/58524303.cms (accessed on 6/1/2017).

68 Adil Rasheed, "Salafi Jihad in Kashmir," http://idsa.in/idsacomments/salafi-jihad-in-kashmir_adil-rasheed_150517 (accessed on 8/7/2017).

69 R. Jagannathan, "Kashmir Is Dead," http://strategicstudyindia-blogspot.com/2016/08/kshmiriyat-is-isis-isation-of.html (accessed on 5/2/2017).

70 Wajahat Qazi, "India's Liberal Intellectual Elite on Kashmir," http://kashmi robserver.net/2016/opinions/indias-liberal-elite-kashmir-obfusccation-or-igno rance-8570 (accessed on 6/7/2017).

71 Radha Kumar, "Kashmir's Unending Tragedy," www.thehindu.com/opinion/lead/kashmiris-unending-tragedy/article18344252 (accessed on 5/1/2017).

72 "Kashmir Human Shield Row," http://timesofindia.indiatimes.com/india/Kashmir-human-shield-row-dirty-war-has-to-be-fought-with-innovative-ways-army-chief-rawat-says/articleshowtoprint/58800274.cms (accessed on 6/10/2017).

73 "Only PM Narendra Modi Can Solve Kashmir Issue," http://times of india.indiatimes.com/india/only-pm-narendra-modi-can-resolve-kashmir-issue-meh booba-mufti/articleshowprint/58556015.cms (accessed on 5/10/2017).

74 "45% Fall in Infiltration After Surgical Strikes," www.ndtv.com/india-news/infiktration-declined-by-45-percent-after-surgical-s (accessed on 10/2017).

75 "Secret Intel Papers Show How ISI Funds Hurriyat," http://timesofindia.india times.com/india-secret-papers-show-isi-funds-hurriyat-times-now/article showprint/58558286.cms (accessed on 5/11/2017).

76 "NIA Starts Probing Geelani and Others for Receiving Pakistan Funds," http://timesofindia.indiatimes.com/india-starts-probing-geelani-and-others-for-receiving-pakistan-funds/articelshowprint5853776.cms (accessed on 5/25/2017).

77 "NIA Continues Raid on Hurriyat Leaders Over Pak-Funded Terror in Kashmir," https://www.business-standard.com/article/current-affairs/nia-continues-raid-on-hurriyat-leaders-over-pak-funded-terror-in-kashmir-117060400228_1.html (accessed on 6/7/2017).

78 Asif Jolly, "Crossing the Red Line," *India Today* (July 24, 2017), pp. 37–9.

79 "India Picks Ex-Chief Dineshwar Sharma to Lead Kashmir Talks," www.hin dustantimes.com/india-news/former-ib-chief-dineshwar-sharma-t-lead-sus tained-dialogue-with-kashmir/story-07fymp8joZUAghSMAX2 (accessed on 11/2/2017).

80 "Hurriyat Rejects Dialogue With Central Interlocutor," https://timesofindia. indiatimes.com/indiahurriyat-rejects-dialogue-with-central-interlocuter/article showprint/61374676.cms (accessed on 11/3/2017).

81 "Nawaz at UNGA: Pakistan Wants Peace With India," www.dawn.com/news/ print/285192 (accessed on 6/7/2017).

82 "Sharif Raising Kashmir With all Leaders Amid Isolation Fears," www.thehindu. com/news/international/Pakistan-prime-minister-nwaz-sharif, and "Pakistan's Bogus Claims Exposed by Own Media in Disastrous Day," http://timesofindia. indiatimes.com/world/pakistans-bogus-claims-exposed-by-own-media-in-disatrous-day/articleshowprint/54469895.cms?null (accessed on 9/30/2016).

83 Vivek Chadha et al., "Uri Surgical Strikes and International Reactions," http:// idsa.in/issuebrief/uri-surgical-strikes-and-international-reactions_041016 (accessed on 10/10/2016).

84 "PM Dispatches 22 Special Envoys to World Capitals," http://nation.com. pk/E.paper/lahore/2016-08-28/page-1 (accessed on 8/30/2016).

85 For the full text of her speech, see www.com/india-news//full-text-of-foreign-minister-sushma-swarajs-speech-at -un-general-assembly-1466709 (accessed on 9/30/2016).

86 "Pakistan's Failed Kashmir Policy," http://thediplomat.com/2016/07/pakistans-failed-kashmir-policy/?allpages=yes&pri (accessed on 6/29/2017).

87 Touqir Hussain, "Are India-Pakistan Relations Doomed," http://thediplomat. com/2017/04/are-india-pakistan-relations-doomed?allpages=yes (accessed on 5/5/2017).

88 "In a Goodwill Gesture, India to Release 11 Pakistani Civil Prisoners Today," http://timesofindia.indiatimes.com/india/in-a-goodwill-gesture-india-india-to-release-11-pakistani-civil-prisoners-today/articleshowtoprint/59099778.cms (accessed on 6/20/2017).

89 Happymon Jacob, "The Story of Two Ceasefires," www.thehindu.com/opin ion/lead/the-story-of-two-ceasefires/article24138555.ece (accessed on 6/20/ 2018).

90 "Indo-Pak Conflict Monitor," http:/ T/164.100.47.4/newrsquestion/showQn. aspx, and htpps://goo.gl/etfbfa (accessed on 10/5/2018).

91 Sameer Yasir and Kai Schultz, "Kashmir Government in Turmoil as Coalition Breaks," *The New York Times*, June 19, 2018.

92 "Report on the Situation of Human Rights in Kashmir," *UN Human Rights Office of the High Commissioner* (June 14, 2018).

93 Kallol Bhattacherjee, "It Seeks to Build a False Narrative," www.thehindu. com/news/national//india-calls-on-report-on-human-rights-abuses-in-kash mir-fallacious/article24166717.ece (accessed on 6/20/2018).

94 "If India Takes One Step Forward, We Will Take Two," *Hindustan Times*, July 27, 2018 (accessed on 8/1/2018).

95 "PM Narendra Modi Congratulates Imran Khan," https://timesofindia.india times.com/india/pm-narendra-modi-speaks-to-imran-khan-expresses-hope-that-democracy-will-take-deeper-roots-in-pakistanarticleshowprint/65203309. cms (accessed on 8/1/2018).

96 "Kashmir Problem Can Be Solved by Embracing People," *Hindustan Times*, New Delhi, August 15, 2018 (accessed on 8/20/2018).

97 Navved Siddiqui, "PM Khan Responds to Modi in Positive Spirit to Resume Talks, Resolve All Issues," *Dawn.com*, September 20, 2018 (accessed on 9/25/2018).

98   "India and Pakistan Foreign Ministers to Meet in Sign of Thaw," *Financial Times*, September 20, 2018 (accessed on 9/22/2018).

99   Ashok Sharma, "India Calls Off Ministers' Meeting With Pakistan," *The Washington Post*, September 22, 2018 (accessed on 9/23/2018).

100   "Pakistan Slams India for Cancelling New York Talks," wwwreuters/reerl. org/a/pakistan-khandenouces-india-cancelled-talks/29504660.html (accessed on 9/24/2018).

101   "It Is Time to Give a Befitting Reply to Pakistan, Terrorists," https://timesofin dia.indiatimes.com/it-is-time-to-give-a-befitting-reply-t-Pakistan-terrorists-army-chief-/articleshowprint65913400.cms (accessed on 9/24/2018).

102   "Dialogue Only Course to Peace," https://pakobserver.net/dialogue-only-course-to-peace-dg-ispr/ (accessed on 9/24/2018).

103   "India and Pakistan Trade Insults After Sideline Meeting Collapses," *The National*, September 30, 2018 (accessed on 10/1/2018).

104   "PM Modi Warns Pakistan of Befitting Reply to Ceasefire Violations," https://timesofindia.indiatimes.com/world/pakistan/pm/modi-warns-pakistan-of-befitting-reply-to-ceasefire-violations/articleshowprint/66021154.cms (accessed on 10/2/2018).

105   "What the Pollsters Found in Kashmir: Bold Questioners, Armed with Pencils, Faced Risks, Got Looks, Learned," *The Wall Street Journal*, August, 14, 2002.

106   "Terrorists Training Camps Making Life Hell," http://timesofindia.indiatimes. com/india/terrorist-training-camps-making-our-life-hell-pakistan-Occupied-kashmir-residents-say/artlceshowprint/54711934.cms?null (accessed on 10/10/2016).

107   "In Koli, Pakistan-Occupied Kashmir Residents Take to Streets Against Atrocities by ISI and Pakistani Army," http://timesofindia.indiatimes.com/world/ Pakistan/in-kotli-pakistan-occupied-kashmir-residents-take-to-streets-against-atrocities-by-ISI-and-pakstan-army-/articleshowprint/54637452.cms?null (accessed on 10/3/2016).

108   "Black Day Observed in POK, Kashmiri Groups Want Pakistani Forces to Withdraw," http://timesofindia.indiatimes.com/word/europe/black-day-observed-in-pok-kashmiri-groups-want-pak-forces-to-withdraw/articleshowprint/ 54999759.cms?null (accessed on 10/ 24/2016).

109   For more discussion on Pakistan's treatment of the POK, see "Pakistan Kashmir," http://freedomhouse.rg/print/39642; Zainab Aktar, "CPEC and the Future of Gigit Baltistan," http://idsa.in/idsacomments/cpec-and-future-of-gilgit-baltistan_zakter_130417; Priyanka Singh, "Severing Gilgit Baltistan's Kashmir," http://idsa.in./idsacomments/severing-gilgit-baltistan-kashmir-link_psingh_190417 (accessed on 4/24/2017), and Behera, *Demystifying Kashmir*, pp. 170–207.

110   "In Kashmir, Nearly Half Favor Independence," http://blogs.reuters.com/ india/2010/05/29/in-kashmir-nearly-half-favor-independence (accessed on 6/13/2017).

111   For more details about the Baloch see, Indurthy, "Pakistan Faces an Uncertain Future," pp. 273–4.

112   "Pakistan Might Ban Blasphemy Laws After 60,000 Killed," November 25, 2015. www.christianpost.com (accessed on 12/1/2015).

113   "Terrorist and Extremist Groups of Pakistan," wwwsatp.org.satporgtp/coun tries/pakistan/terroristoutfits/group_list.htm (accessed on 6/13/2017).

114 "Pakistan Freezes 5,000 Accounts of Terror Suspects," http://timesofindia.indi
atimes.com/world/pakistan-feezes-5000-accounts-of-terror-suspects-includ
ing-that-of-Masood-Azhar/artcleshowprint/55039688.cms?null (accessed on
10/27/2016).
115 "Who Is Killing Pakistan's Shia and Why?" http://warontherocks.com/2014/05//
who's-killing-pakistanis-shia-and-why (accessed on 6/14/2017).
116 C. Christine Fair, "Is Pakistan a Failed State? No," http://foreignpolicy.
com/2010/06/24/is-pakistan-a-failed-state-no/ (accessed on 5/10/2016).
117 Stephen Cohen, *The Idea of Pakistan* (Washington, DC: Brooking Institution
Press, 2004), pp. 69–70.
118 Minihaz Merchant, "How Pakistan Subverts the Indian Elite," www.dailymail.
co.uk/indiannews/article-3441333/how-Pakistan-s (9/26/2016).
119 Hasan-Askari Rizvi, *The Military and Politics in Pakistan,1947–86* (New
Delhi: Konark Publishers, 1988), p. 201.
120 "Double Trouble for Nawaz Sharif as His Brother Also Summoned by Panama
Probe Team in Pakistan," http://timesofindia.indiatimes.com/world/Pakistan/
double-probe-for-naz-sharif-as-his-brother-also-summoned-by-panam-probe-
team-in-pakistan/articleshowprint/59139782.cms (accessed on 6/16/2017),
and Hussain Haqqani, "Pakistan Sticks to a Sad Tradition," www.thehindu.
come/opinion/lead/pakistan-sticks-to-a-sad-tradition/article19391743ece?ho
mepage=true (accessed on 8/2/2017).
121 Asad Hashim, "Pakistan Court Releases Ex-PM Nawaz Sharif and Daughter,"
Aljazeera, September 19, 2018.
122 Arif Malik, "Sharifs Pay Shahbaz Visit at NAB Office in Lahore," www.dawn.
come/news/print/1437434 (accessed on 10/9/2018).
123 Megan Trimble, "The 10 Most Corrupt Countries, Ranked by Perception,"
https://www.usnews.com/news/best-countries/10-most-corrupt-countries-
ranked- by-perception (accessed on 4/14/2018).
124 "Corruption Perceptions Index, 2017," www.dawn.com/news/print/1391129
(accessed on 7/8/ 2018).
125 Harsh Pant, "Imran Khan's Victory in Pakistan: An Outcome Foretold," *The
Diplomat*, July 27, 2018, pp. 1–2.
126 Christine Fair, "Imran Khan: Another Act in Pakistan's Circus," *The Diplomat*,
July 27, 2018, pp. 1–3.
127 M.K. Narayanan, "Making Peace With Naya Pakistan," www.thehindu.
com/opinion/lead/making-peace-with-naya-pakistan/article24849516ece/
homepage=true (accessed on 9/30/2018).
128 Robert Wirsing, India-Pakistan Relations and the Problem of Kashmir, *Indian
Journal of Politics*, Vol. 32, Nos. 3–4 (December 1998), pp. 117–32.
129 Cited in Aiz Haniffa, "Bhutto Regrets Her Hawkish Policy on Kashmir," *India
Abroad*, June 4, 1999, p. 20.
130 "In Extraordinary Development, Pak's Nawaz Sharif Govt Orders Army to Act
Against Terrorists," http://timesofindia.indiatimes.com/world/pakistan/rift-
between-pakistan-government-army-ov (accessed on 10/8/2016), and http://
timesofindia/indiatimes.com/world//pakistan-government-army-over-back
ing-militant-groups-Report/articleshowprint/54726429.cms/null (accessed on
10/8/2016).
131 "Pakistan Army Expresses Concern Over News Leak About Rift With Government," http://timesofindia.indiatimes.com/world/pakistan/pakistan-army-

expresses-leak-about-rift-with-government-/articleshowprint54854839.cms? null (accessed on 10/15/2016).

132 Cited in "Why Can't You Act Against Masood Azhar and Hafiz Saeed?" http:// timesofindia.indiatimes.com/world/Pakistan/why-cant-you-against-masood-Azhar-hafiz-Saeed-pakistan-daily-The-Nationa-daily-asks-islamabad/article showprint/54814221.cms?null (accessed on 10/13/2016).

133 Cited in "Pakistan Has No Tradition of Holding Army Accountable," http:// timesofindia.indiatimes.com/world/pakistan/pakistan-has-no-tradition-of-holding-army-accountable-says-Dawn-editorial/articleshowprint/54864088. cms?null (accessed on 10/17/2016).

134 "Hafiz Saeed Spreading Terrorism in Name of jihad," http://timesofindia.indi atimes.comworld/Pakistan/hafiz-saeed-spreading-terroriam-in-name-jihad-pak-govt/58675168.cms?null (accessed on 5/16/2017), and www.aljazeera. com/news/2017/01/pakistan-hafiz-saeed-house-arrest-170130 (accessed on 1/2/2017).

135 "UN Security Council has Become Unresponsive to Needs of Our Time," http://timesofindia.indiatimes.com/india/UN-Security-Council-has-become-unresponsive-to-needs-of-our-times-indias-strong-reaction-on-Masood-Azhar-issue-articleshowprint/54701957 (accessed on 10/6/2016), and "India Criticises UNSC for Not Sanctioning Masood Azhar," *Daily Pioneer*. www. dailypioneer.com/to-stories/india-criticises-unsc-for-not-sanctioning-masood-azhar.html (accessed on 10/8/2016).

136 Raj Verma, "Pakistan, Masood Azhar and Terrorism," http://idsa.in/idsacom ments/pakstan-masood-azhar-and-terrorism_rverma_150517 (accessed on 5/22/2017).

137 Ayesha Siddiqa, Military Inc, London: Pluto press, 2007.

138 "Pakistan Army Seeks to Hobble Nawaz Sharif, Trip Up India," *Times of India*. timesofindia.indiatimes.com/india/Pakistan-army-seeks-to-hobble-nawaz-shari-trip-up-india/articleshowprint/58567286.cms (accessed on 5/9/2017).

139 Kushwant Singh, "Train to Pakistan" (first edition), New Delhi: Chatto & Windus, 1956.

140 Mohammed Hanif, "India and Pakistan's Dialogue of the Deaf," *The New York Times*. www.nytimes.com/2015/09/03/opinion/mohammed-hanif-india-pakistan-dialogue-of-the-deaf.html?_r=o (accessed on 9/10/2015).

141 "Chapter 6. How Pakistanis and Indians View Each Other," www.pewglobal. org/2011/06/21/chapter-6-pakistanis-indians-view-each-other/ (accessed on 7/8/2016).

142 Rory Medcalf, *India Poll 2013* (Sydney, Australia: Lowy Institute, May 2013).

143 Malik Akbar, "How Pakistan Hurts People by Blaming India," www.huff ingtonpost.com/malik-siraj-akbar/how-pakstan-hurts-its-pe_b_7289882.html (accessed on 6/17/2017).

144 "Pakistan Schools Teach Hindu Hatred," www.dawn.com/news/print/672000 (accessed on 6/3/2017).

145 "What Is the Most Blatant Lie Taught Through Pakistan Textbooks," http:// reddt.com/r/pakistan/what_is_the-most_blatent_taught_through/ (accessed on 9/8/2016).

146 Raja Mohan, "How Prime Minister Modi Can Sustain India's Pakistan Dia-logue," http://carnegieindia.org/2016/02/12/now-prime-minister-modi-can-suatain-india-s-pakistan-dialogue-pub-62707 (accessed on 11/19/2016).

147 Raju Thomas, "Reflections on the Kashmir Problem," Thomas (ed.), *Perspectives on Kashmir*, pp. 3–43.
148 Cited in Victoria Schofield, *Kashmir in the Crossfire* (New York: I.B. Tauris Publishers, 1996), p. 214.
149 "Safe Havens for Terror Groups in Paki Won't Be Tolerated," *The Times of India*. https://timesofindia/indiatimes.com/world/us/safe-havens-for-terror-groups-in-pak-wont-be-tolerated-tillerson/articleshowprint/61231854.cms (accessed on 10/27/2017) and "US Warns Pak: Act Against Terror or We'll Get It Done," http://ahmedabadmirror.indiatimes.com/news/world/us-warns-pak-to-act-against-terror-or-well-get-done/articleshow/61278421.cms?pripage=1 (accessed on 10/30/2017).
150 "Pakistan to Approach IMF for a Bail Out," www.dawn.com/news/1437653/pakistan-to-appraoch-imf-a-bail-asad-umar-announces (accessed on 10/9/2018), and "IMF Warns Pakistan Against Excessive Loans From China," *Dawn*. https://dawn.com/news/print/1438023 (accessed on 10/11/2018).
151 "Pakistan Army Chief Supports Peace Talks With India," *The Indian Express*, December 21, 2017.
152 "Pakistan Army Chief Calls for Meaningful Dialogue to Resolve Disputes with India," ibid., April 15, 2018.
153 Miwaiz Farooq, "Dialogue is only way to Resolve kashmir Conflict," www.dawn.com/news/1448217.
154 Jeffrey Gettleman, "In Kashmir, Blood and Grief in an intimate War," https://www.nytimes/2018/08/01/world/asia/kashmir-war-india-pakistan.html.
155 "Pakistan and India Have Identical Poverty Levels Now," www.thenews.com/pk/print/category/top-story (accessed on 9/10/2017).
156 Sandeep Bhardwaj, "Statesmanship, Not Brinkmanship," *The Hindu*. www.thehindu.com/openion/op-ed/statesmanship-not-brinkmanship/article25265708.ece?homepage=true (accessed on 10/20/2018).
157 "Keep Pak, Out of Picture, Governor Tells J&K Parties," *The Hindu*. www.thehindu.com/news/national/keep-out-of-picture-governor-talks-jk-parties/article25326796.ece?homepage=true (accessed on 10/25/2018).
158 Damodar Sar Desai, "The Origins of Kashmir's International and Legal Status," in Thomas (ed.), *Perspectives on Kashmir*, p. 91.

For Product Safety Concerns and Information please contact our EU
representative GPSR@taylorandfrancis.com Taylor & Francis Verlag GmbH,
Kaufingerstraße 24, 80331 München, Germany

Printed and bound by CPI Group (UK) Ltd, Croydon, CR0 4YY
11/04/2025
01844008-0001